Marketing
for the
New Millennium

Applying New Techniques

Jay W. Tolman

The Oasis Press® / PSI Research
Grants Pass, Oregon

Published by The Oasis Press®
© 1998 by Jay W. Tolman

This publication is designed to provide accurate and authoritative information
in regard to the subject matter covered. It is sold with the understanding that the
publisher is not engaged in rendering legal, accounting, or other professional
service. If legal advice or other expert assistance is required, the services of a
competent professional person should be sought.
> — *from a declaration of principles jointly adopted by a committee of*
> *the American Bar Association and a committee of publishers.*

Editor: Janelle Davidson
Book Designer: Constance C. Dickinson
Compositor: Jan Olsson
Cover Designer: Steven Burns

Please direct any comments, questions, or suggestions regarding this book to
The Oasis Press®/PSI Research:

> Editorial Department
> P.O. Box 3727
> Central Point, OR 97502
> (541) 479-9464
> info@psi-research.com *email*

The Oasis Press® is a Registered Trademark of Publishing Services, Inc.,
an Oregon corporation doing business as PSI Research.

Library of Congress Cataloging-in-Publication Data

Tolman. Jay W., 1954–.
   Marketing for the new millennium : applying new techniques / Jay
W. Tolman
      p. cm. -- (PSI successful business library)
  Includes index.
  ISBN 1-55571-432-3 (pbk.)
  1. Communication in marketing   I. Title
HF5415.123.T65 1998
658.8'4--dc21   97-52778

Printed in the United States of America
First edition 10 9 8 7 6 5 4 3 2 1 0

 Printed on recycled paper when available.

Table of Contents

Preface

The purpose of this book is to provide valuable information and insight to assist individuals with an interest in learning about more effective marketing and advertising techniques. The book provides strategies for combining existing and new marketing methods for greater overall effectiveness. In explaining when and how to use these methods, it details innovative marketing approaches successfully applied in real world situations through actual case studies from three different industries. This book can serve as a text for marketing education as well as provocative reading for business people.

The content provides insights and practical applications for a diverse set of marketing communications methods. These include mass media, sales promotion, direct response, and interactive marketing methods such as the Internet, e-mail, fax, CD-ROM, and interactive kiosks. The information will help the reader more effectively design and implement integrated marketing communication programs that use a broader range of strategies and tactics.

Companies and brands that master the use of these strategies and tactics will be better prepared to compete in the new paradigms of marketing that will come in the new millennium. New millennium marketing will use technology and innovation to provide custom tailored, value-added marketing communication to customers. New millennium marketing will recognize the unique customer differences and preferences for receiving marketing communication. Companies and brands that recognize and embrace these changes will reap the rewards of increased customer awareness, loyalty, and share of customer sales.

Chapter 1

Market for Success

Integrated Marketing

In simple terms, integrated marketing is a holistic approach to using all possible marketing communication tools to build your business. These tools include mass media such as television, radio, magazines, and direct response marketing communication. Direct response marketing includes database marketing, direct mail, sales promotion, telemarketing, and direct response television, print, radio, or Internet and other interactive marketing communication techniques such as e-mail, broadcast fax, fax on-demand, interactive kiosks, and CD-ROM.

For the purpose of discussion in this book, please think of your business as a brand, just like Taco Bell, Toyota, Century 21, or Wrigley's Doublemint gum. The principles of using integrated marketing techniques to build your business are the same as those used to build these large national brands.

During the 1950s through the 1970s, the common paradigm for marketing communications was mass media. Mass media was a readily available,

cost-effective means of communicating with a brand's customers and prospects. It provided some means of targeting different types of customers by using different mass media vehicles. For example, daytime TV reaches women, sports programming reaches men, kids programming reaches children, magazines reach upscale adults, and so forth. Mass media was proven as an effective way to reach large audiences to build awareness and image for brands. The early successes of brands in the packaged goods' industry, such as Wrigley chewing gum, Proctor and Gamble household products such as Tide and Cheer, Coca-Cola, Budweiser, and McDonald's fast food, paved the way for marketers to mimic these success stories; and for the most part, it worked.

During the 1980s and early 1990s, the marketing communications landscape shifted dramatically. First, the cost of using mass media rose dramatically. This was because audiences were more fragmented due to the growth of cable television and other new networks. Networks such as CNN, ESPN, Fox, WBB, and others experienced rapid acceptance and growth. As a result, consumers had many more viewing choices beyond the programming offered by major TV networks, ABC, CBS, and NBC. At the same time, the demand for mass media increased due to many new brands being introduced. However, the number of viewers reached by any given mass media vehicle was lower than ever. The result was smaller audiences, higher prices, and less bang for the buck with traditional mass media as a marketing communication tool.

At the same time this was occurring, computer and telecommunications technologies were rapidly advancing. Some marketers began to explore and embrace new technologies and marketing methods to either replace or supplement mass media as a way to regain or maximize their bang for the buck. These marketers became more aggressive and creative in using different types of marketing methods to increase their marketing results. This included developing databases and using direct mail, telemarketing, sales promotion, direct response TV, print, and the Internet.

Most marketing professionals had expertise in one or two of these methods but rarely more. For example, traditional advertising agencies were proficient at developing mass media advertising only. Database, direct mail, telemarketing, and sales promotion companies were specialists in their own unique marketing communication methods but were not familiar enough with other marketing methods to credibly expand outside of their area of expertise.

For the most part, this continues to be the case today. Large advertising agencies have acquired companies which specialize in direct response and sales promotion. However, these agencies have not been successful in offering this wider array of services to clients. The reason for this is that their primary focus is on mass media advertising while direct response is secondary. As a result, they do not attract the best direct response marketing talent. Many times, the mass media agency personnel are at odds with the direct marketing personnel. In these cases, the two groups have conflicting philosophies and objectives and are competing for a greater share of a client's marketing communications budget. Unfortunately, such agencies do not have marketing personnel sufficiently cross-trained in both disciplines. Many brands should use a combination of various marketing communications methods. However, it is difficult and expensive to effectively coordinate the various marketing tools and specialists into a cohesive, integrated marketing program. Additionally, few marketing professionals have the experience to identify the correct combination of marketing methods to use for a brand.

The intent of this book is to help those of you involved in marketing and advertising for your company to better understand and use a variety of marketing communication methods to improve overall marketing effectiveness. It provides insight, advice, and critical thought processes for more effective mass media and direct response programs. Importantly, the information in this book provides the necessary information to begin evolving your thinking and prepare you for the challenges of marketing in the new millennium.

Chapter 2

Market with Clear Objectives

The Right Objectives

This chapter will provide key information to set objectives for developing an integrated marketing program.

Development of an effective, integrated marketing program must start with a clear definition of objectives and strategies. Just like planning a trip, you start with a destination and a road map of how to get there before packing up the car and driving. The objectives and strategies are multifaceted with one overriding goal, to increase sales and profits.

Here are some important questions and issues to be addressed in developing a sound set of objectives.

- Do you want to increase loyalty among your current best customers to retain them? This requires a clear definition of who are your best customers and what their needs and wants are.

- Is there an opportunity to turn your loyal customers into advocates? There may be a way to motivate them to help you acquire additional customers.

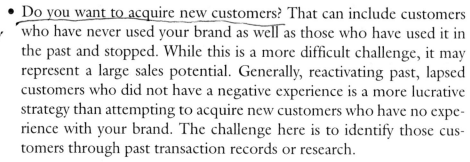

- Do you want to acquire new customers? That can include customers who have never used your brand as well as those who have used it in the past and stopped. While this is a more difficult challenge, it may represent a large sales potential. Generally, reactivating past, lapsed customers who did not have a negative experience is a more lucrative strategy than attempting to acquire new customers who have no experience with your brand. The challenge here is to identify those customers through past transaction records or research.

- Do you want to increase purchase frequency, or repurchase, among a specific segment of current customers? In general, this will be your most lucrative way to spend marketing communication dollars to increase sales and profits. Is there an opportunity to capture a greater share of purchases from customers who use your brand but also use competitive brands? This would require a better understanding of why these customers behave the way they do and how to change their behavior regarding usage of your brand.

An example of this is in the automotive category. Automotive manufacturers and dealers do not know which of their vehicle owners visit dealerships for maintenance and repairs and which do not. Additionally, they do not know which services are being performed at their dealerships versus services at a competitive service provider, such as Jiffy Lube or Midas.

Research results from a random sample of the company's vehicle owners provided a better definition of this sales potential and revealed:

- The percentage of vehicle owners who 1) never, 2) occasionally, or 3) always went to the dealer for maintenance or service,
- Which services they went to the dealer for and which they did not,
- Which non-dealer service providers they used and why, and
- What offers and benefits would motivate vehicle owners to come, or continue to come, to the dealer for more of their service requirements.

This research provided key information to develop informed and focused objectives and strategies. As an example, it resulted in a strategy change from offering loyal customers large service discounts to lower cost value-added benefits. It also provided direction to make more effective offers to motivate prospective customers. Research, whether it be primary, which is done specifically for the task at hand, or secondary, which uses existing data available from a third party, will be the cornerstone for developing the most effective objectives and strategies.

Sometimes targeting a variety of customer segments is appropriate and achievable. Other times, it is more prudent to focus your marketing resources on the customer segment with the greatest potential.

The key to identifying the most lucrative customer segment is establishing a clear definition of the sales potential of each potential customer segment. This is accomplished by using existing information such as sales and research data already accumulated or secondary research such as syndicated research sources or government statistics. In some cases, it is necessary to implement original research to effectively evaluate the sales potential of various customer segment opportunities.

For your own original research, here is one process to follow.

- Determine the total number of customers who have purchased your brand in the past.

- Calculate the past revenue these customers represent and estimate potential future revenue. To find this, you determine the average purchase amount these customers have made in the past.

- Define the purchase cycle, which is how frequently your customers purchase your product or service, monthly, annually, or every five years, for example.

- Assess the customer's past brand loyalty. Within reasonable expectancies for your brand's purchase cycle, compare purchases and dollar amounts for your brand versus the competition.

This identifies the share of customer revenue going to your brand for the various customer segments. It also provides the data necessary to determine very loyal customer segments and less loyal customer segments. From this data you can assign each customer segment priorities, marketing investment allocations, and return on investment projections.

For example, customers who are very loyal, have large revenue contributions, and are profitable are designated as your best customers. Base your budget allocation and marketing communications program upon retaining these valuable customers. You can use various marketing strategies and tactics to reduce attrition and maximize retention of your loyal customers. Then apply the same process to semi-loyal customer segments.

Next, expand the process to prospective customer segments, which are customers who use competitors exclusively. The key information needed to be effective is: <u>what would it take to convert these prospective customers?</u> Then consider how frequent the communication and how aggressive the offer should be. In the automotive category, research revealed that 25 percent of owners of a make of vehicle who use competitive outlets for repair and maintenance could be persuaded to use the dealership with a sweepstakes offer to win a new vehicle. This meant a $140 average purchase could be influenced with an expenditure of pennies per customer.

As data permits, you can develop more sophisticated customer segment analyses. As an example, if statistically reliable data can be applied for various customer segments, you can design a segmentation scheme such as the following.

Customer Group	Brand Aware-ness	Brand Prefer-ence	Average Revenue/ Profit	Return On Invest-ment
Best customers	90%	95%	$140/$70	25:1
Semi-loyal customers High revenue & profit	80%	40%	$140/$70	14:1
Semi-loyal customers Low revenue & profit	75%	37%	$60/$15	3:1
Prospective customers High revenue & profit	30%	2%	$140/$70	25:1
Prospective customers Low revenue & profit	30%	2%	$60/$15	3:1

The most effective marketing programs will generally allow for a variety of marketing communications components. Some of these will be more effective at brand image building; some will be more focused on either building loyalty among current customers or acquiring new customers.

The key to improved effectiveness is analyzing and evaluating all of the marketing communication tools available, then utilizing those most appropriate to achieve objectives and increase overall marketing effectiveness. After prioritizing the customer segments and identifying the

most lucrative customer segment opportunities, the challenge is changing the behavior of those customers to build your brand's market share.

This requires a carefully designed plan including the right positioning strategies, outstanding execution, and the best mix of marketing communication components. These are discussed at greater length in the following chapters.

Chapter 3

Know Your Media and Message

The Role of Mass Media

This chapter provides methods and examples for more effectively using mass media as part of an integrated marketing plan. It addresses three key issues of: 1) how to develop a more effective positioning strategy, 2) how to improve mass media effectiveness, and 3) how to maximize the effective execution of an integrated marketing program.

The primary purpose of mass media as a marketing communication tool has, and continues to be, building brand awareness and creating a brand personality.

Mass media, as a vehicle for building fast awareness, has great merit. After all, not many marketing communications tools can deliver exposure of your brand to 50 percent of the American public with just one commercial during the Super Bowl. Even on a less grand scale, mass media, via prime-time TV, can deliver to very large audiences. A top-rated prime-time TV show can reach 25 to 30 percent of the U.S. households. National magazine publications such as *TV Guide* or *The Reader's Digest* can also reach large audiences in the range of 25 to 35 million readers.

Most advertising professionals would agree that national TV spots are generally more effective at generating awareness and building brand image because TV can offer the three dimensions of sight, sound, and motion. This is in contrast to radio, which offers only sound, or magazines and newspapers, which only offer sight. The pricing of these media vehicles, on the basis of cost per thousand customers reached, will vary accordingly. Television has higher cost-per-thousand prices than radio or print media. Sometimes ad agencies use effectiveness factors to adjust the cost-per-thousand price of each potential media vehicle. These effectiveness factors use research and past experience of the relative impact and effectiveness of each medium. Without these effectiveness factors, the pricing for television is twice as expensive as magazines and 60 to 70 percent more expensive than radio. The effectiveness factors help create a more level playing field for evaluating the cost effectiveness of the various media.

Each media type can be effective; therefore, the appropriateness of each media type is evaluated relative to your brand objectives and strategies.

There are three key factors for more effective use of mass media: the right positioning strategy for the brand, effective media expenditures, and outstanding execution.

The Right Positioning Strategy

Since the early days of advertising, the conventional wisdom has been that customers have a limited capacity to comprehend and retain brand names and brand benefits. For a brand to be successful in reserving a place in the customer's mind, it must be able to provide a unique and relevant reason for being. This requires the proper research to identify what motivations drive your customers. Your understanding of these motivations provides critical information to position the brand as a more desirable alternative than competitors.

The major U.S. advertising agencies early on created philosophies around brand positioning. Each agency had its own twist, which it promoted as unique and superior.

Ted Bates created the unique selling proposition philosophy of advertising. The idea of this philosophy was that the strategy must focus on a real or perceived benefit that a brand possesses and which makes it a superior choice for customers. The advertisement, first and foremost, must clearly register this unique selling proposition. This philosophy spawned campaigns such as Charmin's Mr. Whipple and squeezably soft, as well as many other notable campaigns for Procter and Gamble's household products.

Ogilvy and Mather professed that "Telling isn't selling; the customers must like the brand before they will buy it." This philosophy leads to strategies and executions which go beyond simply registering the brand benefit or unique selling proposition. This approach includes building a favorable image or personality for the brand so the customer will relate to, and have an affinity for, the brand. The American Express "Don't Leave Home Without It" campaign is an example of what came out of this philosophy.

Leo Burnette's philosophy was based on building brand imagery and preference through relevant and memorable characters as spokespersons. Examples of these campaigns produced the Pillsbury Doughboy, Charlie the Tuna, and the Jolly Green Giant.

The J. Walter Thompson Agency's philosophy is stimulus response. The stimulus response philosophy professes that the content and tone of an ad must be designed to elicit the desired response from the customer, the response which will most effectively achieve the brand objectives. The strategy focuses on desired customer response or, in the customers' viewpoint, what they sense, what they feel, and what they know about that brand.

For example, here is the desired customer response for Kraft American cheese singles.

Sense	Feel	Know
Kraft singles look and feel like a higher quality than the private label brands.	I trust Kraft's quality, and I feel more comfortable giving better quality to my family.	I know that Kraft is the best; buying Kraft means giving my family the best I can, even if it costs a little more.

With this philosophy, advertising emphasizes achieving the desired customer take-away or response to the actual advertisement. The advertisement's content and tone are important only inasmuch as they are successful in achieving the desired response. Each component of the ad works to achieve the desired customer response, including the photography or film style, actors, locations, props, music, and announcer.

Each of these agency's philosophies contains valuable critical thinking avenues for applying brand positioning strategy. The most effective strategy will be a hybrid approach, incorporating the best of these philosophies. An example of a brand positioning strategy structure to accomplish this is given here.

Objective

What are the marketing objectives? What are your priorities in building sales and profits? You might list here such statements as to acquire new customers or triers, retain existing customers, generate repurchase, or capture a greater share of customer purchases.

Strategy

You want to position your brand with all the selling propositions that make the brand unique and superior. First note the unique benefits or attributes the brand possesses that give the customer a reason to believe that the brand is superior.

Second, think about the brand personality. Write a brief statement about the brand's desired personality or image that will make it more relevant and memorable to customers. Words like professional, trustworthy, fun loving, adventurous are often used to describe the desired imagery for a brand.

Then consider customer take-away. What is the desired customer response to the ad?

Consumer Research

All agency philosophies and approaches use consumer research in some way or another. The following procedures give an ideal research path for developing effective strategy and execution. That's not to say it will be practical or realistic to your situation, given time and budget limitations. However, an understanding of the ideal process will help you to make better informed decisions on where to take shortcuts.

A market structure audit seeks to obtain the customer's perceptions about where a brand fits in with the way they shop for products or services. This research technique provides customer information about which brands compete, in the mind of the customer, and why. This can sometimes be quite a different view than that of the manufacturer. A market structure audit allows customers to arrange the competitive landscape and the choices and tradeoffs they make when considering purchase of your brand. A study like this can provide better insight into how to position your brand more effectively in the marketplace. Sometimes there are some real surprises.

For example, a market structure audit the Wrigley company did for chewing gum revealed that the bigger positioning opportunity for their chewing gum brands was in competition with flavored candy, breath mints, Certs, and Tic Tacs. In many cases, customers were looking for a convenient way of freshening their breath, and they would choose between chewing gum and breath mints. This had a profound effect on their positioning strategy. The positioning of several Wrigley brands shifted to breath mints as the competition, as opposed to other chewing gum brands.

A problem detection study seeks to get the customers to articulate and identify problems they have with your brand and competitive brands.

One of the easiest things to discover in consumer research is the customer's dislikes. Everyone is a critic at heart. When given the opportunity to articulate complaints, customers will give you all you could possibly want or need. The results of a study like this allow you first to quantify which problems are the most significant to customers. Second, it allows you to determine if your brand can be repositioned as a solution to a problem customers may have with a competitive brand. Third, it provides information about what can be done to improve your brand to overcome problems you may detect in the study.

An example of how this worked for the Wrigley Company was in the positioning of the Big Red brand. The problem detection study indicated that Dentyne customers disliked the portion of the gum being small and the flavor not lasting long enough. Big Red customers had neither of these complaints. This led to Big Red being positioned as a better alternative for customers who chew Dentyne. The campaign that resulted showed a visual comparison of a stick of Big Red and a tab of Dentyne along with the slogan "No Little Cinnamon Gum Lasts as Long as Big Red — Last a Little Longer with Big Red." This campaign has run since the late 1970s and continues today. It effectively increased Big Red's market share at the direct expense of Dentyne.

A concept sort is a research method that develops alternative one or two-sentence strategy concepts for customers to rank. The customers' rankings indicate the positioning concepts which would be most persuasive to them. The customer force ranks eight to ten concepts, from most favored to least favored. Rankings include competitive brand concepts to better gauge the effectiveness of new alternative brand concepts, versus your current competition. Additionally, the study covers various customer segments including current loyal customers and competitive brand customers. This is a good technique for new products as well as established brands.

The Ken-L-Ration dog food division of Quaker Oats provides a good example of how concept sort research helped invent the Kibbles 'N Bits brand. Concept research indicated that customers — the owners, that is, not dogs — preferred feeding their dogs a combination of traditional dry, crunchy food called kibbles with softer, semi-moist food called bits. At this time, these two types of dog food were sold separately, and customers had to mix them together on their own, which many did. Based on this research, Kibbles 'N Bits was formulated and positioned as a more convenient alternative for these customers.

Brand image mapping analyzes that critical component of the brand's positioning strategy, its brand image or personality. Identifying the correct brand personality relative to competition can have a significant impact on marketing effectiveness. Establishing the right brand personality as part of the positioning strategy is an important component of the guidelines or blueprint you use to develop all marketing communication tactics.

After you establish the most effective personality or image for your brand, all marketing communication tactics should accurately reflect this. Their consistent look and tone will be most effective in establishing your brand in the customer's mind. This image makes it easier for the customer to recognize and recall your brand's relevancy and thus influence purchase decisions.

It is more art than science to establish the right brand image. The key lies in first truly understanding the qualities and attributes that customers value most, then evaluating which of those qualities your brand can realistically claim.

Techniques used to establish brand image range from focus groups to very expensive quantitative studies. Many times the information already exists through previous research and market knowledge. Qualitative research, such as focus groups, refine and validate your theories of the right brand personality, which is the personality that will project the desired imagery to customers. The case studies in Chapter 5 provide actual examples of how this was effectively accomplished in the restaurant, automotive, and real estate industries.

Testing communications tactics measures the efficacy of an actual TV commercial or print ad. Generally at this stage of the development cycle, there is already a high level of confidence in the basic message. These research techniques then help determine whether the ad is effectively communicating the desired strategy message and whether it is effectively influencing the customer's purchase decision.

There are several companies that have established methods for conducting this research. McCullom Spielman is one that is widely used. They and others seek to replicate a real world television viewing environment to evaluate TV commercial effectiveness prior to spending millions of dollars airing the campaign. They do this by recruiting random samples of customers to evaluate new pilot TV programs. Prior to seeing the TV program, the customers are given a baseline survey to measure their attitudes and preferences about various brands, including yours. The customer watches the television program, with commercials, just as they would expect to in a normal viewing. The customer fills out another survey after the viewing which measures recall, attitudes, and preferences. This survey provides data for the commercial's effectiveness in changing attitudes and preferences for the brand. The commercial receives a series of scores. These scores are compared to a data bank of hundreds of other TV commercials tested the same way. The commercial's relative performance is measured by comparing this data.

Communications tactics research is used to test a finished, produced commercial, or a good facsimile, of the proposed final commercial. Sometimes two or three alternate campaign approaches are surveyed at the same time to determine the best executional approach. The research results provide feedback to make changes and improvements to an executional approach, as well as providing measures for go or no go decisions.

An example of how this research paid off is with Century 21 real estate. After considerable research was completed to set the most effective positioning strategy, communications tactics were tested with several campaign approaches. Alternative campaigns were presented in the form of art boards on video tape to provide a good facsimile of the proposed commercial. Voice-overs, music, and motion effects were added using computerized video techniques to provide rough commercial concepts. This process allowed Century 21 managers to select the most effective approaches and make refinements prior to final production. It resulted in final commercial test scores that were more than 100 percent above average. The campaign performed similarly in the actual marketplace by increasing sales 20 to 25 percent.

In-market testing is the ultimate method for evaluating a campaign's effectiveness when the stakes are high and budgets are sufficient. This consists of airing one or more campaigns in different markets for a period of time. Actual sales results of the campaigns are compared in the various markets. The sales results provide the critical data to make decisions about the alternate campaigns. Additionally, surveys are conducted to measure the effect of each campaign on awareness, attitude, and brand preference.

Taco Bell provides an example for the effective use of in-market testing. The popular Run for the Border campaign had been airing for a couple of years. To plan ahead, Taco Bell and its ad agency prepared alternate campaigns as potential replacements for Run for the Border. The purpose was to explore new approaches that may achieve even better results than Run for the Border, even though Run for the Border was continuing to deliver strong results.

An alternate campaign, using the same basic brand positioning as Run for the Border, aired in three geographically-dispersed markets, while Run for the Border continued in the rest of the markets. Taco Bell had high hopes and expectations for the alternative campaign, and at one point, even considered replacing Run for the Border without the benefit of a test. More rational minds prevailed, however, and the test was conducted. The result was that Run for the Border out-performed the alternative test campaign by a large margin. Run for the Border continued to air nationally, and the alternative campaign was scrapped.

Note the important lesson inherent here. Sometimes marketing managers who are closely involved in the advertising process form emotional preferences and use these as a basis for decision making. It is critical to obtain and use customer input in making decisions on advertising. It is the customers' opinions that count. At times, there may be other factors which cause decisions to be made that are not completely consistent with research results. However, all the facts are known prior to making those decisions. For more information on how to do low cost market research, see *Know Your Market* by David Frigstad.

Effective Media Expenditures

Experience indicates that most major advertising agencies use very similar media strategies and tactics for their clients. A client does not decide which advertising agency to use for their brand based on an agency's media creativity. When media is a factor in the decision as to which agency to use, it is usually based on an agency's media buying volume and clout in the marketplace. For example, one agency may have large client budgets and marketplace clout for spot television and another for network TV sports or prime time programming. Agencies will argue that their marketplace clout provides better media pricing for a client.

There are some instances in which creative media planning or buying can make a profound difference for a brand. The following examples demonstrate this point.

For Jovan fragrances, a young and aggressive media planner was able to execute two creative media ideas that extended the client's media budget and gave them a significant increase in their bang for the buck. This occurred only because the media planner was invited to become a full member of the team, which gave the agency media planner a better opportunity to understand the client's business and marketing strategy. Here is how it paid off for Jovan.

Jovan was an upstart fragrance company with a limited advertising budget relative to its competition. Yet the major retailers insisted on high-impact advertising in order to distribute and promote Jovan's line of fragrances. Jovan decided to concentrate its limited ad budget in the top 25 markets to demonstrate that they had high-impact advertising. They would do this through buying many TV spots in less expensive day parts like early and late evening, with an occasional spot in prime time. The spots were heavily weighted to the pre-Christmas gift-giving season, and to the extent possible, prior to Mother's Day and Father's Day, the other peak gift-giving seasons.

Through some careful analysis, the media planner discovered some interesting facts. For instance the top market spot television prices during the pre-Christmas season were disproportionately high relative to network TV for the same time of year. This was due to the demand of local retailers in these top markets for local TV time during this crucial retail sales period. In fact, the cost of buying spot TV in the top 25 markets was nearly the same as buying network TV, which covered the entire country. In network TV the week just before Christmas, prices dropped dramatically because most major national advertisers were selling their goods two to eight weeks in advance of Christmas. Also, fragrance was a last minute gift purchase, usually by men for their wives, girlfriends, or mothers. The second highest sales period for fragrances was the week after Christmas when retail gift returns and bargain shopping were at their peak. Network TV prices drop by an additional 40 to 60 percent for the week after Christmas when national advertisers' demand was low.

Jovan achieved the equivalent of 35 percent more advertising coverage without spending more by shifting a portion of media expenditures from the top 25 markets. They shifted two of the spot TV weeks to network TV the week before and after Christmas. The programming they bought was during higher quality prime-time Christmas specials and prestigious football bowl games. Jovan's ability to merchandise this higher impact TV plan to retailers was instrumental in securing additional distribution opportunities.

At the same time, several new ideas emerged. Jovan fragrance customers were youthful men and women, ages 16 to 34. These are customers who are active, on the go, and up late at night. This became the foundation for a network TV strategy that was focused in the late night daypart that attracted younger viewers of the Tonight Show, Saturday Night Live, Friday late-night concerts, and Late Night with David Letterman. This daypart programming became Jovan's key media strategy to merchandise with retailers as high-quality, high-impact advertising that was national in scope and would reach all customers in all of a retail chain's stores.

Thus, Jovan was able to effectively show their retail customers, the chain store's fragrance purchasing manager, that it now had a media schedule that was national in scope and supported all of the key seasonal periods like Christmas, Mother's Day, and Father's Day. It made the statement that Jovan had arrived into the big time.

There was one final stroke of good fortune that increased the impact of Jovan's media program. Since TV networks were eager to attract advertising dollars, there was intense competition between the networks to get new network advertisers. With this in mind, Jovan's media department approached NBC with a novel idea. The proposal was for Jovan to place three commercials in a given night on the Johnny Carson Tonight Show several nights each year prior to the peak fragrance seasons on condition that Johnny Carson do a live mention of Jovan as a new sponsor just after his nightly monologue. NBC and Johnny Carson agreed. The result was a carefully orchestrated method for Johnny to make the live mention for Jovan. The ad agency hired the sexiest women in Hollywood to dress in provocative swimsuits to carry the Jovan product to Johnny on stage for the mention. Johnny used the opportunity to make this a big finale to his monologue. It was 60 to 90 seconds of Johnny being Johnny, with this sexy model and the Jovan product center stage. It was one of the funniest moments of the show every time it occurred, and Jovan benefited by getting additional air time that was extremely valuable.

Another good example of effective media spending through creative media and positioning strategy was the Joseph Schlitz Brewing Company. At the time, Schlitz had just hired the J. Walter Thompson Agency to attempt to save this very troubled brand. In the two or three years prior to this, Schlitz had had serious sales slides, losing its number one market share position to Budweiser.

There were two key reasons for the decline. One was that Schlitz, in a cost-saving move, changed the brewing process for its flagship brand. Unanticipated problems occurred, and loyal Schlitz customers began to defect. The second was when Schlitz reverted back to the original brewing process, then gave the incumbent Leo Burnette agency the task of creating a new campaign to win back Schlitz customers. It resulted in a hastily-crafted campaign placed on national TV without the benefit of adequate prior research. The campaign was a disaster. It featured macho-looking men such as lion tamers aggressively urging customers to buy Schlitz. This series of commercials became known as the "Drink Schlitz or I'll Kill You" campaign. It further offended beer drinkers, including past and present Schlitz customers.

J. Walter Thompson (JWT) took over to accomplish a turnaround — a long-shot in the marketing world. JWT conducted a range of research and discovered that, even though the Schlitz brewing process had reverted to the original method, beer drinkers continued to believe that Schlitz did not taste as good as their newly adopted brands, such as Budweiser and Miller High Life. JWT did additional research which revealed that loyal Budweiser and Miller High Life drinkers preferred Schlitz by a margin of two to one, when the brands were compared in blind taste tests.

JWT created an innovative and bold campaign, the live Schlitz taste tests. JWT purchased two-minute blocks of time during half-time of the NFL playoff championship games and the Super Bowl. JWT set up a live taste test in each of the cities where the games were being played. A set was built to seat a panel of 100 loyal Budweiser or Miller High Life customers. A real NFL referee was hired to officiate the taste test, and special handles were placed in front of each beer drinker. The plan was to place unmarked glasses of Schlitz and Budweiser or Miller in front of each beer drinker, with the handle in between the glasses. After tasting each glass, the beer drinkers were instructed to move the handle in the direction of the beer they preferred. At center stage a large football scoreboard registered the final tally of the brand that the beer drinkers selected. The scoreboard told the whole story. In these live taste tests, Schlitz won every time by a two-to-one margin.

The taste test results were placed in newspaper and magazine ads following each live taste test event. The ads were rushed to major newspapers and weekly magazines, such as *Sports Illustrated*, *Time*, and *Newsweek*. The ads ran immediately, due to a previously negotiated arrangement, hitting newsstands within 48 hours after the live event.

As a follow-up, JWT created a TV campaign featuring beer drinkers with a pronounced loyalty to either Budweiser or Miller High Life participating in another live, blind taste test. The camera filmed their tasting and their reaction when they were told they selected Schlitz over their brand.

Showing loyal Budweiser and Miller customers, representing a large percentage of beer drinkers, actually preferring the taste of Schlitz made powerful advertising.

The campaign was a big success. Sales trends turned positive, and Schlitz regained market share. Just as this miraculous turnaround was occurring, Stroh Brewing purchased the Joseph Schlitz Brewing Company. The reason for Stroh's purchase was to acquire Schlitz brewing facilities around the country in order to expand the Stroh brand from a successful regional brand to a nationally-distributed brand. Stroh's management discontinued advertising support for the Schlitz brand. As a result, Schlitz fell into oblivion. Today, Schlitz can rarely be found in a grocery store, restaurant, or tavern.

Given the right planning and chemistry, creative media planning can have a tremendous impact on marketing communication effectiveness.

Commercial Length

There are other strategies to get more bang for the buck out of a marketing budget. For example, a mix of standard 30-second commercials and shorter length commercials, such as 10 or 15-second spots, can extend a budget substantially. Media pressure is increased by as much as 50 percent by using shorter length commercials. This is due to 10 and 15-second spots being priced at half of a 30-second spot.

When using this approach, it is important to ensure that creative strategy is effectively implemented in a shorter length. Most can be just as effective, despite the ad agency's protest. It is more effective to schedule the longer 30-second spots early in the media schedule so the shorter spots build off the exposure customers have already received. In some cases, it may be advisable to design a shorter commercial independent of the longer 30-second commercial. However, it is usually a relatively simple matter to edit a shorter length commercial when done at the onset of designing a campaign.

Research has demonstrated that a 10 or 15-second commercial can be 85 percent as effective as a 30-second commercial. At half the cost, this adds up to substantially more bang for the buck. In some cases, 10 or 15-second commercials have been successfully used as a total replacement to 30-second commercials. This is appropriate when the shorter length commercials communicate the strategy as well as the longer ones. This is not a common occurrence, but it can happen. The media impact doubles when this strategy is implemented.

Scheduling to Support Sales Seasonality

With media time being such an expensive commodity, a common and prudent strategy is to schedule media to support the highest seasonal sales periods for a brand.

As an example, in real estate, the majority of home buying and selling activity occurs in the first half of the year. This is because families want to be in their new home prior to the new school year starting. Consequently, media is scheduled at moderate levels during January through March to lead the season. During this period customers are beginning the mental process of preparing for this important move, absorbing critical information such as which real estate companies they will interview. The heavier media spending is concentrated during April through July, when the actual decision-making process takes place.

In an industry with little seasonality, media budgets can work harder by concentrating in lower cost quarters such as January to March and June to August. In these quarters, demand for television air time is lower, and prices reflect this with considerably lower cost.

Up-front versus Scatter Purchasing

With the television medium, large advertisers must evaluate the marketplace each year to determine whether to commit the budget up-front or purchase quarter by quarter. The key issue is whether or not the overall price is better negotiated by committing the majority or all of the budget prior to the year beginning. This would be in anticipation that demand for air time will be strong over the next year and that prices will be higher for those who purchase later. These decisions can result in either saving 10 to 15 percent, or paying 10 to 15 percent more, depending on market conditions.

The quality of the programming purchased will also be somewhat dependent on whether the purchase is up-front or quarter-to-quarter. Higher-rated programs are more available when purchasing the schedule up-front. This is an important consideration because research has indicated that higher-rated and more popular programs achieve greater recall of your commercial among your customers. The higher recall may not be dramatic but should be factored in as part of the price value equation.

Opportunistic Purchasing

Give serious consideration to maintaining a reserve fund for opportunistic purchases throughout the year. These opportunities will usually present themselves a day or two before the program's air date. When this occurs, it is because there are spots available that, if unsold, will not produce revenue for the station. To avoid a total loss, the station will seek last-minute buyers and sell the air time at a 40 to 60 percent discount on the original price.

Sponsorships

For a high-impact strategy, brands will sometimes purchase sponsorships in high-profile programs, such as awards shows, the Super Bowl, all star games, the Olympics, or the last episode of a popular TV show. Generally, brands pay a premium to purchase several spots in these programs, and they sometimes receive on-air sponsorship mentions. This can be an effective strategy to introduce a new brand or to kick off the key selling season.

Outstanding Execution

With the right positioning strategy and a cost-effective media plan in place, the process is half-way completed. The one thing that has been learned over and over in the marketing world is that the best strategy in the world will not succeed without outstanding execution.

I once attended a marketing seminar given by Tom Bonoma from the Harvard Business School. Mr. Bonoma's specialty is marketing execution and its importance to success. He has written books and lectured around the world on this subject. Our group spent two full days with

Mr. Bonoma who taught us about the importance of execution and demonstrated its value through case studies from some of the leading marketing organizations in the world.

Our group took Mr. Bonoma's teachings to heart and set out to accomplish one of the finest execution processes in modern marketing history. It was the Taco Bell value initiative in which an integrated marketing approach was used to communicate the key, unique benefits Taco Bell had recently engineered, lower prices, quality product, and convenience.

Shortly after this experience, I was reading a bedtime story to my son, which made me realize how simple the notion of outstanding execution is. The book I read to my son was a Bert and Ernie Sesame Street story. The story was about how Ernie, the more inept of the pair, came up with the idea to have a lemonade stand. Ernie announced his idea to everyone on Sesame Street and invited them to the opening. Then with Bert's help, Ernie began making all the arrangements for the stand. First, he went to the market to buy lemons, but instead of lemons he bought oranges. So Bert went to the market to exchange the oranges for lemons. When Bert returned home, he discovered that Ernie had completely botched the painting of the sign for the stand. So Bert made a new sign. This continued on, where Ernie would botch things and Bert would fix them. When the lemonade stand opened, and it was a big success.

Everyone on Sesame Street complimented and praised Ernie for having such a great idea. Naturally, all the praise Ernie received hurt Bert's feelings since he had done all the work. He corrected all of Ernie's mistakes and actually made the idea of a lemonade stand really work. Bert couldn't take it anymore and began to cry. He said, "Sure it was Ernie's idea to open a lemonade stand, but I had to return the oranges for lemons, I remade the sign, and Ernie gets all the credit. It's easy to have an idea, but it's not so easy to make it work." This fundamental lesson about the importance of execution, first touched on by the Harvard professor but which came through crystal-clear in a children's book, has stuck with me ever since.

Attention to detail and follow-through in the implementation of a strategy and program are vital to its ultimate success. As the proverb says, "There's many a slip 'twixt the cup and the lip." This idea of the importance of outstanding execution is discussed and expanded upon in the case studies in Chapter 5.

Chapter 4

Connect with Your Customers

The Role of Direct Response

This chapter provides explanations for the key direct response strategies and methods. It addresses when and how to use databases, direct mail, sales promotion, telemarketing, direct response print, direct response TV, the Internet, e-mail, fax services, interactive kiosks, and CD-ROM.

Direct response marketing communication goes beyond building awareness and image by providing a mechanism for customers to respond to the communication and start a dialogue with your brand. Customer responses can range from requesting more information about a brand to actually completing a transaction. The type of product or service and the purchase cycle of the brand will dictate the type of response mechanisms you use. By creating a customer dialogue and providing an opportunity for the customer to respond instantly through the response mechanism, you make it easier for the customer to form a stronger bond with your brand. The result is that direct response is more effective in changing behavior among customers.

The behavior you seek to change through these forms of marketing communication will range from increasing perceived customer satisfaction and loyalty for a brand to getting customers to purchase a brand.

In the past, marketers have thought of different direct response strategies and tactics within a very narrow range. Typically, a single tactic was used to accomplish a single task. Examples of this are banks which used direct mail to cross-sell additional products to their customers. For example, if customers have checking accounts, the bank would use direct mail to persuade them to buy a certificate of deposit. Banks have used a giveaway sales promotion tactic, such as a free small appliance, to entice prospects to open a new account.

Other examples are credit card companies using direct mail or telemarketing to increase card ownership. In real estate, local offices will send continuous direct mail letters to establish and maintain a relationship with homeowners in the hopes that when it is time to buy or sell a home, they will get the assignment.

A key reason for the limited scope and use of direct response approaches has been the lack of understanding and expertise among marketing practitioners about a broader range of direct response methods. Most marketing professionals have expertise and a comfort level in only one or two direct response methods. Direct mail companies stick to direct mail; telemarketing companies offer only telemarketing services; sales promotion specialists stay within the confines of their expertise. The result has been lots of specialists but few professionals and companies capable of effectively integrating a variety of direct response methods to support a brand. In reality, many components of direct response methods can be used together.

Clearly, direct response is not appropriate for all types of brands. The brands which are most suited will possess one or more of these characteristics:

- Your brand includes more expensive, higher-ticket products and services. This does not necessarily exclude inexpensive products and services if they are purchased frequently or in large volumes by a segment of a brand's customers. However, the overall sales and profit potential for a brand must justify the expense of direct response marketing communications.

- Your brand has a variety of narrowly-defined customer segments for which customized positioning strategies and communications would be more effective than one general message.

- There is an opportunity to have an ongoing dialogue with customers to create a better bond with them and increase brand loyalty.

- Your management desires better accountability of marketing expenditures and a more definitive analysis for return-on-marketing investment.

- There is a need to use a unique marketing method to more effectively break through the communication clutter in reaching customers.

Much has been written recently about the value and importance of new marketing techniques to get, keep, and develop customers. Marketing pundits have referred to these techniques as relationship marketing, loyalty marketing, retention marketing, one-to-one marketing, and targeted direct response marketing. The process and techniques are fundamentally the same, even though many different names have been used. The key principles are based on the fact that technology now permits marketers to communicate with customers with more relevance and specificity in a custom-tailored way.

The principal technology which enables this new form of marketing to be more effective than traditional mass communication marketing is the advancement of computer processing technology. Computer technology allows you to build databases of customer names, with a virtually endless capacity to include detailed information about each customer. Information that allows you to understand the needs, wants, and motivations of each separate customer makes it possible for you to develop highly customized communication programs for different types of customers.

A customized conversation will create a tighter bond of loyalty between the customer and your brand. The conversation is two-way and involves the customer. The process seeks to truly understand the unique needs and wants of each customer and then tailors the conversation based on that deeper understanding.

The customer and your brand both win in this new paradigm of marketing. The customer gets more meaningful and relevant information while you achieve greater loyalty, increased responsiveness, and return on marketing investment.

Few marketing professionals would argue with the fact that the new marketing techniques of direct response marketing are superior to the old marketing methods. The old method was a shotgun approach with a general message blasted via mass media in hopes that it would reach as many customers as possible.

As mass media audiences diminish and advertising costs increase, marketers must embrace and perfect one-to-one marketing approaches. There is little doubt that the future of marketing will gradually shift toward a greater investment and use of these new techniques.

The technology and techniques now exist to allow marketers to take a much more segmented and customized approach to communicating with their customers. However, only a small percentage of companies have done so.

Companies who do utilize these more advanced marketing techniques will achieve a greater return on their marketing investment. The most sophisticated companies are relying on specific consumer behavior, as measured through their transaction databases, to identify very specific customer characteristics. These customer characteristics are used as a basis for grouping customer segments or clusters. Then two-way communication systems are developed to ask consumers additional questions to help further refine the segmentation approach.

The critical steps in the process are as follows:

- Collect and format data.
- Create specialized customer clusters.
- Develop and implement custom-tailored marketing programs for customer acquisition, loyalty, referral, and repurchase.
- Track the marketing programs.
- Evaluate results.
- Refine your methods.

You have a key opportunity to further improve marketing programs through a one-to-one relationship marketing approach. Applying these strategies and approaches involves analyzing the motivational drivers of customers, then using this information for highly customized marketing communication that is targeted to each customer.

Insurance and real estate companies, for example, have successfully developed an array of customized communication programs that are more relevant than one general communication approach would be.

The way this has worked for insurance is to send messages to existing clients that seek to retain them as customers and sell them additional services; other messages generate qualified leads or appointments from prospective customers. All communications seek to establish the company's products and services as more relevant to the individual. Considering motivational drivers, an insurance company will send a marketing communication to young families that focuses on a recognition and empathy of their need to provide protection and security for their children. To pre-retirement adults, the focus is on how the company's products and services can help prepare for a secure retirement.

Real estate companies have designed programs which define distinct segments of sellers and buyers and then vary the communication to each. A strategy for past customers who have been in their home for five or more years and have a new addition to their family would suggest, "Trust us again to show you how you can buy a larger home without increasing your monthly payment." To first-time buyers, the message is, "Now you can own your own home for no more than you are currently paying for rent." In each case, the list of names used for mailing is carefully selected and prequalified based on a number of criteria.

Generally, the data is plentiful for successfully accomplishing custom-tailored, one-to-one marketing. Relatively inexpensive modifications to a basic format, usually through laser imaging, help create these customized communication programs. The intent of this book is to provide ideas and hands-on direction to those marketers interested in immediate use of these techniques for their organization.

The following sections will provide detailed information to assist you in designing and implementing state-of-the-art database marketing programs. The methods for accomplishing this include direct mail, sales promotion, telemarketing, direct response television, print, Internet, e-mail, fax, CD-ROM, interactive kiosks, and a marketing communications database. The emphasis here is on a better understanding of how to use a combination of these methods. Ultimately, this will result in designing and implementing more effective integrated marketing programs.

Integrated Direct Marketing Fundamentals

In this section you will learn how to design and implement the fundamental components of an integrated direct marketing program. You will see how each component should be designed so that all the brands marketing communications work together in an integrated fashion. When you integrate the various components, you will have an overall direct response program that is consistent with your mass media program for building brand image. It will also supplement the mass media program by allowing you to open a dialogue between a brand and its customers. This dialogue will collect customer data, which you can use to more effectively provide customers with value added communication. This more customized conversation creates brand loyalty.

The end result of this process will be your having marketing communication programs that work in unison to enrich the quality of the customer information in your database, thus improving the marketing communication program to your customer.

The Database

Think of the process of developing your database as building a new medium, like television, radio, or magazines. However, when you build this new database medium, you define exactly with whom you want to communicate. Imagine no waste; you reach only those customers you want to, at the frequency you choose. You create the so-called programming or editorial to appeal to small portions of your customer base, thus ensuring that they will fit one another just right.

Creating many smaller segments of your customer base and giving each segment the programming or editorial they want will result in each customer being more interested, responsive, and appreciative. It is as if you are taking an open book test where the questions are very simple.

These are some objectives you can use to guide the process of developing a database.

- Develop statistically reliable, reasonably-sized customer segments. To be statistically reliable the segment size should be a minimum of 1,000 customers and, when possible, a minimum of 5,000 customers. The importance of the customer segment size being large enough to be statistically reliable is to be able to measure behavior changes caused by marketing. Larger sample sizes provide greater confidence levels that the customer behavior change was attributable to marketing, rather than random chance.

- Include routine updating so there is a built-in emphasis on keeping information as current as techniques and data allow. One example of this is updating customer data by regularly submitting the database to a service vendor that is able to use postal service data to update address changes. Another example of this is the automotive business which updates customer repair order information in order to facilitate timely mailers to customers to remind them just before their next service is due.

- Establish a procedure to assure the validity of the data so customer segments are based on a solid foundation of accuracy. One effective way to do this is to regularly survey a random sample of 125 to 150 of the customers in each segment. The survey would obtain purchase behavior information and other customer data to ensure that the premise and definition of each customer segment is accurate and valid. For example, if the survey results from a random sample of a loyal customers segment revealed that their recent purchase behavior did not follow a loyal customer definition, the integrity of the customer segment would be questioned and corrected.

- Develop a process that allows easy transition to the next level of customer segmentation.

- Provide a means by which you can readily access your data to develop appropriate strategies and tactics.

As a broad overview of the possible ways that database segmentation is applied in actual programs, look at the following automotive example.

For a more detailed discussion of the three phases for approaching the database development process, see Chapter 6.

Hypothetical Automotive Cluster Segments

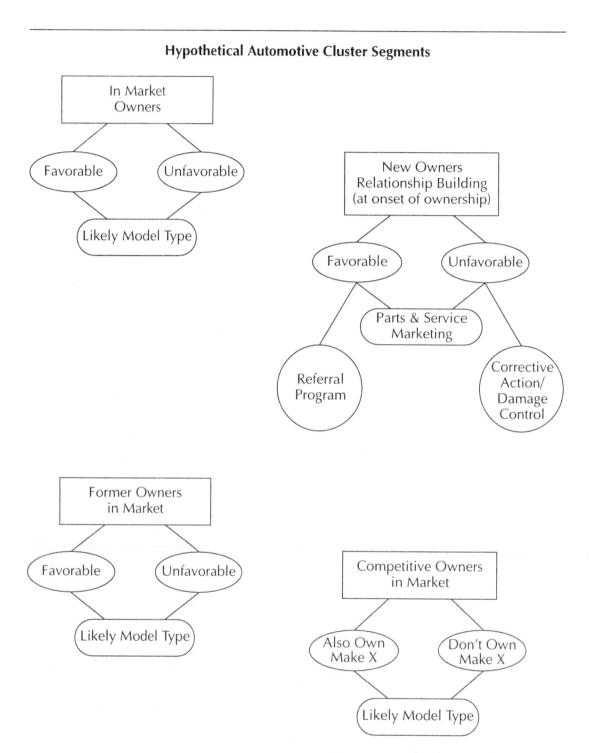

The possible variables to be used to determine additional customer segments are endless. They can include additional variables as described below. The variables used to create separate and distinct customer segments are based on judgment, experience, and statistical analyses. A dynamic process of continued analysis and testing will help ensure your customer segments to be more specifically defined and effective.

Possible Variables to Determine Customer Segmentation

Data Variables

- Lease expiring
- Own for X years (analyze owner file and purchase cycles)
- Mileage
- Annual repair order dollars
- Total # service visits
- New birth
- Household income
- Loan close to payoff
- Other demographics
- Psychographic profiles

Most Likely Type of Vehicle

- Existing makes and models owned
- Immediate previous make and model owned
- First-time buyer
- Family size
- New birth
- Income
- Education
- Past make owned
- New vehicles purchased

Disposition Toward Make and Model

- Satisfaction scores
- Dealer proximity
- Vehicle make owned
- Owned make in past

Promotion Responsiveness

- Past promotions
- Test offers

Direct Mail

Direct mail becomes a critical communication method in the overall marketing mix. Think of it not in the old paradigm of junk mail but as a high-tech method of delivering custom-tailored marketing communication to different segments of customers.

Direct mail is the workhorse in the communications mix because it can be an inexpensive means of sending relevant messages to the right customer at the right time. With the foundation of a carefully built database, which includes well-defined customer segments, direct mail is a means to send highly personalized messages to customers, messages inexpensively tailored to each customer's need, wants, and motivations. You control the communication frequency and timing, based on the criteria set to reach each customer segment. As an example, a relationship marketing program to retain a brand's best customers could have a greater frequency than a program targeted to acquire trial among new customers. Communication frequency and message content are varied based on the marketing budget available to target a range of customer segments.

The most effective direct mail program, in terms of customer response, will have the optimal combination of the right list, offer, and creative package. The right list is a composite of customer information acquired from a variety of sources, such as transaction records, research, lists or data purchased from third-party sources, and a carefully-designed customer segmentation scheme. Because the list component of the program will determine 50 to 60 percent of direct mail's effectiveness, it is clearly important to invest the resources to get this component right.

The right offer in the direct mail program will determine 30 to 35 percent of its effectiveness. Identifying the most motivating and cost-effective offers through research, analysis, and testing is also very important. More detail on offers is provided in the sales promotion section to follow.

The creative message and package will account for the remaining 5 to 20 percent of the program's effectiveness. Although the creative message and package are less critical than the list and offer in driving customer response, they deserve strong attention to maximize response and to build the brand's awareness and image. Historically, the role of direct mail has been a response-generating marketing method while its contribution in building and enhancing brand image was neglected. With an integrated marketing paradigm, direct mail creativity is more important. The role of the creative component takes on greater importance to maximize the investment in direct mail. Direct mail is a media vehicle that supports brand awareness and image as well as generates customer response. Therefore, the direct mail package should be designed using the brand positioning strategy to ensure it accurately reflects the brand's selling proposition and personality.

Customer research provides good insight into the most effective direct mail creative approaches. These findings lead to different approaches than have historically been used by direct mailers. Customers have busier and more hectic lifestyles than ever before. Many families have both parents working full-time outside of the home. As a result, they have little time to spend sifting through and reading their mail. These customers have become very savvy about sorting out irrelevant junk mail or mail that is too difficult to comprehend. Customers want direct mail advertising that is brief and to the point, with no fluff or wasted words. This leads to creative approaches that are more graphic and simplistic in style, such as simple self-mailers, postcards, or other methods that quickly and clearly register the brand and offer benefits.

Customers have also developed a more discriminating eye for direct mail advertisements. They are very adept at identifying mail that does not appear to have a quality appearance. If a direct mail piece is low quality, customers will not open the package. As customers have said in research, "This kind of mail is quickly identified as junk and goes right into the trash."

There is a flip side to this. If a direct mail piece has a quality look and contains useful, relevant information, customers will devote the time to reading it. This leads to such creative approaches as newsletters written with customer input to make the content relevant and interesting.

Customers recognize and appreciate when you have invested the time and resources to create a quality direct mail piece. They view these pieces as value-added, thus improving impressions of your brand. Customers have said that, "When I see a direct mail piece that has a quality look to it and has relevant, helpful information, I feel the company cares about me. If the company sending the mail piece has taken the time to understand my needs and invests the resources in doing it right, I'll read the piece and see it as a value. If it is not, I'll see it as a come-on and throw it away."

The process of creating effective direct mail programs is relatively complex, and much has been written about creating effective direct mail. Rather than restate this, the following will highlight the critical information for you to be aware of and understand.

Personalization

Direct mail creative packages should always have the customer's name in the address panel. This is the first thing the customer will look at when opening the mail. If the address panel does not have their name, spelled correctly, it will be a signal that the mail is not valuable but rather is junk mail. This is especially true for address panels that have current resident or any other generic type of reference to the addressee. The more personalized the mail piece, the more the customer will view the communication as relevant and meaningful. This includes the salutation in the letter inside the envelope carrier and creative techniques to maximize the personalization. An example of this is designing a newsletter that features the customer's name as part of the banner or headline.

Return Address

The second element the customer will read on a direct mail package is the return address. If the return address indicates a company with whom the customer has not or currently does not do business with, it will more than likely be perceived as irrelevant. Consequently, it is better to use a generic return address when targeting prospective customers when there is not an existing relationship or connection to the brand's name.

Postage

The third thing noticed by the customer is the postage mark on the direct mail package. Customers are savvy about postage rates and terms. They know a postage meter mark on the package is likely to indicate a mass mailer. Additionally, if the postage rate is below first class, it is likely to be perceived as a mass mailer. Whenever possible, avoid having the direct mail package appear to be a mass mailing. Customers want to feel special and cared about, and a personal touch will accomplish this better than a mass production approach. The more the direct mail package appears to be a personal communication to the customer, the more likely they are to open it. When using third class bulk rate postal rates for direct mail, a third class postage stamp, rather than an indicia, will create a more personal impression. Bulk rate stamps can be designed to have the appearance of first class postage, and the stamp looks more like a personalized piece of communication.

Response Mechanisms

It is always a good idea to provide at least two options for the customer to select from in responding to a direct mail piece. A toll-free 800 number will generally be more cost effective and allow for a faster, more immediate response. However, research has demonstrated that using only an 800 number may reduce response rates dramatically. When customers were given two options for responding to a direct mail program, the options being an 800 number or a business reply card, customers chose the business reply card 85 percent of the time. Most customers feel it is easier and more convenient to respond by mail rather than telephone. However, a significant number, 15 percent, would rather pick up the phone to respond. By using both an 800 number and business reply card, response rates are maximized.

Compared to other direct response methods, direct mail will continue to have broad customer reach. Therefore, design your direct mail programs so they more effectively collect customer information, maintain an interactive dialogue, and integrate with your use of other marketing communications methods.

Sales Promotion

Sales promotion activities include sweepstakes, contests, refunds, discount offers, and coupons. Sales promotion can also include premium offers, sports marketing, and event marketing. Traditionally, marketing professionals have used sales promotion as a tool to provide a short-term lift in response or sales. Well-designed sales promotion programs also provide added value benefits to your brand, such as enhancing its awareness, image, preference, and database of prospects and customers.

As a starting point, here are some guidelines for assessing the opportunity for using sales promotion in your marketing program.

- Can a sales promotion help increase consumer awareness and break through the clutter?
- Can it increase response to the program or provide a response lift?
- Can it enhance the way customers perceive the product or service?
- Can it provide a means of building a database by collecting additional demographic or product usage information?

The following are some basic components in designing the right sales promotion program.

- Make the offer relevant to the consumer and to the product or service. For example, it probably would not be relevant for an automobile manufacturer to design a sweepstakes that gives away a sailboat instead of a new car.

- Design the sales promotion concept so that it extends or enhances your core marketing and communications objectives. Prudential Real Estate, for example, had an objective of positioning their service to upscale customers. Consequently, they purchased a sponsorship in a very upscale competition, The America's Cup, as a means to borrow the prestige image of this event. The goal was to build an association between Prudential and The America's Cup and elevate Prudential's image. In addition to meeting this goal, sales promotion tactics surrounding The America's Cup event, including trips to the event, generated prospect leads and helped build a database.

It may be appropriate to design several different sales promotion programs for different target segments. Century 21 real estate identified three different target segments, each with separate sales promotion components that were uniquely relevant.

Renters or First-time Buyers

For renters who were potential first-time home buyers, two sales promotion components were used. First, a free set of real estate guidebooks were offered to these customers. The guidebooks included valuable information such as what to look for when buying a home, the pros and cons of various finance programs that were available, and how to prepare for moving from one home to another. These books recognized this customer segment's need for unbiased information to make them more comfortable in pursuing a home purchase.

The second sales promotion component was a sweepstakes to win $21,000 for a down payment on a home. This recognized the key barrier many first-time home purchasers face, of not having the money for a down payment. The sweepstakes provided an offer relevant to first-time purchasers that would motivate them to consider the possibilities of home ownership.

Move-up Buyers

For move-up buyers, those customers who already owned a home but desired a larger home or a better location, two different sales promotion components were used.

The first was a free extensive cleaning of a customer's current home for anyone who listed their home for sale with Century 21. The second was a sweepstakes to win free mortgage payments for a year when the customer purchased a move-up home through Century 21. This recognized that the main barrier for this customer group was their concern about larger monthly payments when purchasing a more expensive home.

Satisfied Customers

For satisfied customers who had recently purchased a home using a Century 21 agent, the company used a different sales promotion tactic. It was a sweepstakes to win a free year of air travel for referring a friend who was interested in buying or selling a home. This recognized and rewarded the satisfied customer while providing an incentive to generate qualified customer leads.

Sales promotion is a relatively cost-effective way to provide added value to your overall marketing plan. It can build awareness, image, preference, and response rates while providing an additional tool to enhance a database. The key is to always keep the strategic purpose of the sales promotion in mind throughout the development and implementation process.

Inbound Telemarketing

The use of a toll-free number in virtually any communication vehicle can provide many benefits. It provides an easy, convenient way for a customer to respond to a marketing communication. It allows for an orderly, systematic way to respond to customer information needs and requests. It provides a means of tracking customer responses to various sales tactics by using a variety of 800 numbers. A toll-free number will also be an excellent method for collecting valuable customer information to build and enhance a database. This data can be used to create customer segments for future customized direct response communication programs.

There are several types of telemarketing techniques that can be applied to your marketing program to make them interact more effectively with customers. The three basic 800 number inbound telemarketing methods are live interface, direct connect, and automated fulfillment.

In a live interface method, a consumer calls an 800 number and is connected to a live operator who asks a series of questions and fulfills the caller's request, whether for information, to order a product, to get the address and phone number of a local outlet, and so on. Frequently, the questions asked of the consumer help qualify them as prospects, so that name, address, demographic, and usage behavior information is collected for future marketing efforts.

Live interface can also be a sophisticated technique to screen prospects before forwarding them to the local dealer. Telemarketing services can store databases of various distribution points in order to forward the lead to the appropriate place, usually done by fax within 2 to 24 hours.

Direct connect methods use a pre-programmed database list of dealers to automatically forward a call to the appropriate dealer. The caller enters their zip code and is matched to the most appropriate dealer, using a zip code database. Another option is a switching station method by which a caller, based on telephone prefix, is automatically matched with a dealer, based on prefix and geographic proximity. The latter approach is used when less precise geography is required to match up a caller and dealer and when one dealer serves a very broad geographic area, such as an entire town.

An automated fulfillment method, for programs that are relatively simplistic, is designed primarily to provide information, such as a brochure, through the mail. This method is relatively inexpensive. As with direct connect, the caller's phone number is recorded and can be used to get names and addresses to enhance a database.

There are pros and cons to each method. Live interface is more expensive but allows for gathering better data and screening the caller. It is also slower in ultimately connecting the caller to the dealer. For example, although it may take 2 to 24 hours for the dealer to receive a fax, there are potential delays after that, such as in the dealer following up with the customer. Direct connect provides telephone number capture, from which 75 percent can be reverse-matched to get names and addresses.

This is more limited than the live interface, and there is some prequalification, or assessment, of the quality of the lead. With direct connect, the customer is put in touch with the dealer more immediately.

Outbound Telemarketing

Outbound telemarketing has received a bad reputation in recent years. Customers become annoyed by these unsolicited sales calls to their homes or businesses and have a negative attitude toward them. However, research indicates that customers would appreciate telemarketing if done responsibly and appropriately. When outbound telemarketing is part of an integrated marketing program, studies show it can increase response by as much as 40 percent.

This type of telemarketing can be costly, and if used improperly, can backfire by alienating customers. There are few existing guidelines to evaluate and plan the use of outbound telemarketing as part of an integrated marketing program. The most effective approach is to evaluate and apply the use of this marketing communication tool relative to your brand objectives and strategies. The case studies in Chapter 5 provide useful critical thinking and insight into how some brands have effectively integrated outbound telemarketing. You can use these examples as a basis for deciding whether to use outbound telemarketing.

Direct Response Print

The easiest way to think about direct response print is that it is a direct mail ad with a response mechanism that is inserted into a newspaper or magazine for broader exposure. Direct response print has advantages and disadvantages relative to direct mail.

One advantage is that the mass exposure of a publication helps to provide a lower cost per exposure, that is per person reading the publication, relative to most forms of direct mail. Another advantage is that lifestyle and special interest publications may provide a better predisposition to an advertiser's message. For example, a boating magazine ad by a finance company that offers a $2,500 loan for a speed boat would effectively reach customers who are receptive to the subject and offer. Mass print also helps to build awareness and image among secondary and tertiary target segments for possible future targeted direct response marketing efforts. For ethnic marketing, specialized ethnic publications, such as *La Opinion*, provide a means to reach ethnic groups with customized information, without suggesting that they do not understand English. Second or third generation American ethnic customers often are fluent in English and may resent a mailer in their mother language.

The disadvantages are that some advertisers may view the mass exposure of a publication as waste exposure, that is, reaching individuals who may never be prospects. Also, an ad in a mass publication is exposed in a cluttered environment compared to direct mail. A prospect may never notice an ad in a publication but can hardly miss a piece of mail. Additionally, it is more expensive to personalize an offer or message than in direct mail.

If you are considering the advantages and disadvantages of direct response print, it is important to know that publications may offer lower direct response rates to advertisers, as they do in the broadcast media. Ad rates for nearly all publications are highly negotiable.

Direct Response TV

You can use television advertising to create interaction and response between your brand and customers. As a strategy or tactic in an overall marketing plan, direct response TV, called an infomercial, can provide several benefits.

One benefit is that an infomercial provides a long format to communicate complex messages. The longer format provides the opportunity to build awareness, image, and preference, while including a call to action that generates a lead or a sale. Infomercials are an especially good way to generate excitement, enthusiasm, and interest among both your consumers and your internal constituents such as your agents, dealers, or brokers. It can also serve the role of modeling positive behavior to the sales force.

Another benefit is that infomercials are an excellent means to provide a controlled demonstration of a product or service and are a relatively low-cost way to use the television medium. Also, infomercials can be a means of adding qualified prospects to your database for other direct mail programs.

If you decide to use direct response TV, you can ensure your success by including in your infomercial certain critical components. It should have a format or story line that allows for an interesting, entertaining way to convey information over a 30-minute period. It should also have a strong call to action which motivates the target audience to call an 800 number or visit a dealer. The call to action should include a relevant, compelling offer, such as a contest, sweepstakes, discount coupon, free premiums, or valuable information. To facilitate easy, convenient access to the offer, the infomercial should repeat the 800 number with each call to action, usually three to four times during the program. The infomercial's strategy, tone, and message should fit with the overall marketing program of your brand in order to convey a consistent image.

It is a good idea to plan some research testing of your infomercial. You can use focus groups or test markets prior to producing and airing the infomercial on a broad scale to ensure the program's effectiveness.

Once your infomercial is ready to air, you will need to know something about media purchasing. Infomercial time can be purchased on nearly every local TV station and most cable stations. Infomercial time is sold by a separate sales staff. Infomercial time is usually available only in off-peak periods such as weekends, late night, or early morning. Each network or local station will have a different definition of off-peak. For example, the Discovery Network considers 3 A.M. to 9 A.M. every day as off-peak. But the local CBS station airs its morning program from 6 A.M. to 9 A.M., and infomercials are generally not available. As a rough guideline, the rates for a 30-minute infomercial are inexpensive and highly negotiable, depending on supply and demand. Media rates for direct response TV, infomercials and two-minute and one-minute direct response TV commercials, are often one-third or less the price of traditional image spots.

The following are a few more basics of infomercial media buying. These also apply to two-minute and one-minute, direct response formats.

Commercials are purchased and rotated within broad time segments called dayparts, such as the daytime daypart from 10 A.M. to 4 P.M. Commercial spots are generally run at various times during this broad time range. The spots will air on a random rotation basis, unless a fixed time position is negotiated, usually at a higher cost.

Direct response television commercials are pre-emptable. Often, in a high demand quarter of the day such as the fourth quarter, the greatest challenge is having your schedule actually run as planned without substantial pre-emptions. Payment for direct response television is made up-front before the schedule runs.

The infomercial and direct response TV industry is undergoing explosive growth and change. Consequently, the way things are today may be different in six months or a year. The changing and growing nature of the industry has also created a situation in which there are few real experts. Those who truly are must constantly adapt to rules that can and do change frequently. Recognizing this reality is important. It's not a negative but rather a fluid environment to understand.

Internet Marketing

Marketing on the Internet has become a popular topic. The future prospects for this media are very promising. Estimates by various professional organizations predict the majority of homes in the country will be connected with the Internet by the first part of the new millennium. Many companies have already begun experimenting with Web sites. Most are merely preparing for when the Internet will become a common media vehicle. However, for the most part, that day has not yet arrived. Only a few companies are effectively using this medium now. Information here will help you evaluate the potential use of the Internet as a marketing communications tool.

Using the Internet as a marketing or media vehicle is the same as any other direct response marketing vehicle. Since parallels with direct response TV are the most relevant, applying the fundamentals of direct response TV will result in more effective Internet marketing. Design your Web site using the same objectives and principles as direct response TV. The following will discuss how to do this.

First, it is important to understand that the Internet exists to provide helpful, accessible information to users. Customers use the Internet to acquire useful information to help them with a particular need. Therefore, it follows that customers' needs should determine the objective and design of a Web site. This sounds fairly elementary, but many of the brands now using the Internet do not consider this. Many companies become enamored of the Internet as an exciting new billboard, and consequently their ad design has little strategic direction. The key issue is whether your brand has relevant information for customers to access.

Using the Internet well can provide further support to your brand positioning and customer relationships.

As in direct response TV, a good Web site is a way to establish customer dialogue with your brand. This is ideally accomplished through research or existing market knowledge to identify the key, relevant needs the customer might seek from a Web site.

For example, a real estate Web site is created to provide valuable information to help buyers and sellers in the complex real estate process. This may include information on how to determine the price of home for which they can qualify, how to make their house more salable, or how to select the right real estate company to assist them in the process.

When Web site content is presented from the customer's perspective, customers will appreciate it and begin to develop favorable impressions toward a brand. It is important that the Web site design makes it easy for customers to quickly spot information relevant to them. It should also be easy for them to access the information. This means limiting Web site content to only the most relevant and important topics. Many companies develop Web sites that are far too ambitious and cannot resist the temptation to include lots and lots of information. This will work against them because of the great degree of Web site clutter that exists and customers' lack of time and patience to sift through it all.

The design of the Web site should be intriguing and attractive to hook Internet browsers. However, be careful not to go overboard when using graphics. Some Web sites have elaborate and beautiful graphics, but customers have a harder time opening these sites and become frustrated with slow transmission rates. One day this will not be a barrier when more homes have access to high speed data transmission lines. Now, however, most customers rely on telephone lines for data transmission, and it is a slow process to transfer elaborate and complex graphics.

The Web site should feature a prominent and easy-to-use response mechanism. This might be a brief questionnaire to collect customer data or an actual ordering mechanism, where appropriate.

Your Web site response mechanism should also collect customer data in order to develop a database of these interested individuals with important demographic and brand usage information. This data will be easier to collect if the Web site includes an offer to customers. An offer can range from free information or free product samples to contests or giveaways. This will more effectively establish a dialogue and relationship with customers and provide a method to separate Internet browsers from buying customers.

Another purpose of the customer response database is to track purchases resulting from the Web site exposure. This will enable calculating return on investment for the Web site as separate from other marketing tactics.

An important part of a successful Web site is promotion of the Web site address and benefits to customers. Without an effective promotion program, it is unlikely that many customers will visit a Web site. There are a variety of means to accomplish this. The most obvious method is to promote the Web site in all of your brand's marketing communication materials including direct mail pieces, point-of-sale merchandising, print advertising, and packaging.

Other methods of promoting a Web site are advertising it in the on-line and Internet access services such as Prodigy, America On Line, Microsoft Network, Netscape, and CompuServe. Also, list the Web site with major search engine and directory services, such as Yahoo!, Lycos, and Excite. Agreements with other relevant Web sites to cross-promote one another is the most cost-effective promotion.

When customers who actively use the Internet are identified, consider using the Internet for additional follow-up communication to these customers. An example of this is in automotive service reminder programs. When a customer has indicated a preference toward electronic communication, it is logical to send automotive service reminders via the Internet or e-mail rather than by traditional direct mail. You will help increase brand loyalty when you customize communication methods based on the customer's preferences.

E-Mail

Electronic mail continues to grow in acceptance as a communication method. The uses of this communication vehicle are focused in two areas, business correspondence and customer communication.

In business correspondence, many companies and individuals rely on e-mail as an important means of communicating. Surveys show that 85 percent or more of all businesses use e-mail. The type of communication is very flexible. It can include simple messages to individuals or groups.

Memos, presentation documents, and newsletters can be transmitted quickly. The medium can be either a closed-ended system that is set up exclusively for a specific group of individuals, such as within a company, or it can be over the on-line services such as America On Line or the World Wide Web. When the medium is on-line services or the Web, an address book of individuals is created for easy access to the individual or groups of individuals to whom you wish to communicate.

In addition to general communication, you can also use e-mail to quickly transmit press releases, pricing and product changes, and a variety of other information you would ordinarily send via fax or mail. The disadvantages are that not everyone is diligent about reading their e-mail on a timely basis. Therefore, you cannot always ensure that your information is being received. When this is the situation, you will have to have a secondary back-up system of communication. This will typically be a fax or hard copy via mail.

In any case, e-mail provides a convenient means of transmitting information and an easy way for people to respond to your communication. Since the communication can be close to real time, it is an excellent way to facilitate interaction.

As for customer communication, electronic messaging communication is growing in use and acceptance. Some of the early adopters of this form of communication have been companies that focus on selling their products and services through on-line services or through the World Wide Web. The examples of this are too numerous and varied to summarize. It is relatively easy to use as a sales tool. However, the skepticism about the types of products and services that are sold using this method is a barrier. It is sometimes difficult to evaluate the credibility and quality of the sponsor, and customers have serious reservations about the privacy of the information they provide through a computer. Consequently, the success of this communication method as a means of transacting business is limited.

Fax Services

Broadcast fax and fax on demand programs can be important elements in your integrated marketing communications program.

A broadcast fax service allows you to communicate with hundreds or thousands of individuals quickly and simultaneously. Broadcast fax programs are used in business to business applications. Nearly all businesses have fax capabilities so the total reach of the fax as a communication tool is very high. A fax sent to another fax machine results in production of a hard copy communication that can include modest graphics. Since the fax medium sends and produces hard copy communications, it is quickly noticed, read, and acted upon. A written confirmation of successful transmission to each fax number is also provided.

One application of a broadcast fax is in communicating with regional sales staff, field managers, or key customers. A broadcast fax may be used to provide urgent announcements and updates to large, geographically separated groups of individuals. The types of information communicated are typically price or product changes, new product or service announcements, and miscellaneous news.

Another application of broadcast fax is for research projects. It is most appropriate for self-administered surveys when fast response turnaround is necessary. Fax survey research is typically used as a substitute for a survey distributed through the U.S. mail. It can improve survey distribution and response time by two to four weeks. This is based on a mail survey print production and first-class postal delivery time of five to seven days compared to fax production and transmission time of a few hours. With a fax distribution method, the respondent is more likely to return the completed survey via fax. This may result in survey response analysis within days rather than weeks.

There are some cautions in using this method of survey distribution and response. First, carefully select the audience for the survey. That is, the audience should be involved and have some interest in the subject of the survey. Additionally, the audience should be able to quickly understand that their response will be beneficial to themselves in the long term. This tends to be more relevant with business-to-business survey research. It is especially true when the responders are motivated to provide information to help the sponsor of the survey to improve products, services, or pricing.

As an example, a large national supplier of fire truck parts and services surveyed fire chiefs nationwide. The survey was designed to determine needs, wants, and behavioral data relative to fire truck parts and service purchases. In this particular case, the fire department personnel had a strong interest in helping suppliers to achieve better parts and delivery methods because they were not satisfied with existing methods and suppliers and felt improvements would make them more productive in serving the public. The survey was received and returned via fax, which made the whole survey process faster.

Secondly, you may need to offer an incentive of some kind to motivate respondents to complete and return the survey. The incentive can be monetary, an entry into a sweepstakes, or a charitable contribution. In the fire department survey, an incentive for returning the completed survey was a donation to the American Red Cross made on behalf of each fire department that returned a completed questionnaire.

Fax on demand is used to provide fast, customized information to customers. When customers call a toll free number to receive technical support or sales information, a pre-recorded message guides the customer through a series of touch-tone prompts. The pre-recorded message and the customer's responses, through the touch-tone pad, navigate through a wide assortment of topics. When the appropriate topic comes up, the customer is prompted to provide their fax number to receive the desired information. Within a matter of seconds, faxed information is transmitted to the customer.

Fax on demand is used extensively by computer, printer, and electronic company customer support operations. These companies use fax services to supplement their technical support personnel.

In setting up and implementing a fax on demand service, consider the customer's preferences for the service method they receive. Some customers appreciate the efficacy of the fax on demand service while others prefer speaking directly to a customer support representative. Whenever possible, offer customers a choice of live interface or automated fax customer service delivery. This will ensure a more positive customer service experience that will increase brand loyalty. Also, when designing the fax on demand customer interaction system, consider ways to make the process fast and convenient. Some customers may not appreciate having to devote a lot of time to get the answers to their questions.

Fax on demand could be used as a means of stimulating new ideas and applications in your business. Rather than just using it as a customer support tool, think about how else it may be applied to create interactive relationships with customers. As is the case with all new forms of technology and interactive marketing techniques, businesses today are only just scratching the surface of possible new and creative applications.

Interactive Kiosks

Kiosks are another new application of technology to create an interactive dialogue with customers. Interactive kiosks can take many forms and, with imagination, can be used in many different ways.

Interactive kiosks consist of a branding element such as a sign, indicating the sponsor and purpose of the kiosk. Additionally, kiosks will have a technical component that allows the customer to receive valuable, relevant information while at the same time providing relevant information about them. The technical component can be a computer, a silicone chip, or a telecommunications device. The important thing is that it capture and provide information cost effectively.

In many cases, an interactive kiosk can look and function like a three-dimensional web site. Imagine a kiosk application from an automotive manufacturer that is described here. An automotive company set up a site in a shopping mall. The site included a display of one or more new vehicles for potential customers to see, touch, and feel. The interactive technical aspect of the kiosk offered customers the opportunity to price the vehicle and to price various option packages customized to their own taste. It also provided a video virtual test drive experience.

The customer benefits from this type of interactive marketing experience because it makes the car shopping experience spontaneous, convenient, and low pressure. The customer is allowed to experience the vehicle and learn about its features and pricing, at their own pace.

The brand benefits from increased awareness and trial and the valuable customer data that is captured. Data that can be used to create a profile of the types of customers who are attracted to the vehicle includes customer's name, address, telephone, existing vehicle information, and planned or future buying intentions. This data is used to create a follow-up program inviting interested customers to the dealership for a test drive.

An example of a different type of interactive kiosk is an independent and freestanding automated display powered by a computer chip. The display has the ability to read magnetic cards and communicate visual or vocal messages to customers. It also captures personal data as encoded in each customer's personalized magnetic strip.

One example of an application for this type of interactive kiosk is for a soft drink company. Customers were sent a direct mail promotional package that announced a promotional event that was occurring at all participating grocery stores. The mailer directed customers to visit the brands' display and to use a personalized customer card at a special mechanism at each display. The customer, by using their card, received prizes and discounts. The prize was awarded instantly and vocally communicated to the customer by the programmed computer chip in the display.

The kiosk provided a unique experience to customers that added value to their relationship with the brand. The uniqueness of the promotional technique provided many display and merchandising opportunities for the brand. The kiosk also provided a great deal of valuable customer data. At the end of the promotion, the kiosk computer chips were collected. The chips had gathered information about each customer who participated in the promotion, such as which stores they shopped or how many times they participated in the promotion. This database of information provided a proprietary list of customers who were motivated by this type of promotion. The list was used to target future promotions for the same brand and for other brands marketed by the company. This became a unique way to develop a strategy of interactive promotional programs targeted specifically to customers most responsive to these tactics. This was used as a sales generator and brand loyalty builder.

CD-ROM

CD-ROM represents a communication method using digital techniques as a way to communicate with customers and provide value-added benefits to the customer relationship. A CD-ROM program should be designed for user relevance and friendliness. While the benefits of this technique are pleasing graphics and interactive applications, the meat of the offering should be to make the customers life easier in one way or another.

An example of this is found in the automotive category. CD-ROM disks can be given to customers of a particular vehicle make and model. The purpose of the disk is to allow vehicle owners to keep track of vehicle maintenance and repair. The customer inputs their driving patterns, in the form of average annual miles driven, and the disk provides a custom-tailored service reminder program for the customer to use. The program will automatically prompt the owner when certain services are due, such as oil changes, minor and major scheduled maintenance, and tire rotations.

The sponsor of the disc can program special service offers that are prompted by the reminder program, as an added value to the customer and a way to secure the service transaction. Other digital elements can be included, such as color maps showing their location, hours of operation, and telephone number.

The use of a CD-ROM as a communication tool and value-added benefit to customers is limited only by the designer's imagination. Some of the things to consider when designing a program are to make the CD-ROM format in both PC and non-PC formats and to offer the program in a diskette format for those individuals not having CD-ROM capabilities. This will allow the program to be used by all customers without alienating anyone due to their hardware capabilities.

When you consider the design and development of an integrated direct response marketing communication program, review all of the possible strategies and tactics available in the context of how they will help meet your objectives. Additionally, explore ways to apply the content developed for one tactic to other tactics. Make sure each marketing tactic is consistent with your brand image and with the type of information you want to collect for enhancing your database.

If you follow these guidelines, you will have a more effective, integrated marketing communication program. This will assure that all strategies and tactics are being applied in a consistent, systematic way to achieve a common set of marketing communication objectives.

Chapter 5

Apply Integrated Marketing Principles

Introduction

This chapter will discuss how integrated marketing principals were applied successfully in three real world examples in the real estate, restaurant, and automotive industries.

In each case example, you will get to see the entire process of research, objectives, strategy, program design, implementation, and tracking. The intent is to demonstrate effective integration and application of all the principles and information provided in the previous chapters.

The most effective process in developing an integrated marketing communication program for a brand begins with a thorough understanding of its customers. This can be accomplished using existing research, customer surveys, and focus groups or with other techniques and resources, and the case studies will demonstrate many of these.

After you research customer needs and purchase behavior, you can then set clear and measurable objectives. The objectives are important because you will use them as guidelines for developing all your marketing communication strategies and tactics. You then design all strategies and tactics according to how well they help you meet objectives.

The process of strategy and tactic development and refinement is continual. As strategies and tactics are put into place, carefully track and measure their effectiveness so you can continue the successful ones and change or discard the less successful ones.

Throughout this process, you will note there is much emphasis placed on continually gathering and updating customer information for your database. The database of information is essential for improving strategies and tactics. Conversely, the strategies and tactics are designed to continually gather up-to-date customer information to enhance the database and thus improve programs.

Real Estate Case Study

This real estate case study demonstrates the use of a fully integrated marketing and advertising program, incorporating positioning strategy, mass media, infomercials, direct mail, telemarketing, sales promotion, the Internet, and public relations.

The processes and programs described illustrate the successful re-positioning of the Century 21 brand. The result of this re-positioning was a 25 percent improvement in sales trends.

During the 1970s and early 1980s, Century 21 real estate grew at a rapid pace. Through franchising, the company expanded to more than 7,500 real estate offices nationwide. Because the franchise agreement called for each office to contribute a fixed percentage of gross commission income to a national advertising fund, the Century 21 brand had a strong advertising presence.

By 1985, consumer awareness of the Century 21 brand was above 90 percent. This ranked it as a household name, much like McDonald's or Coca-Cola. Additionally, research indicated that consumers had a very strong pre-disposition to use Century 21 if they were to buy or sell a home. More than 21 percent of all consumers expressed a preference for Century 21. This was 10 times greater than their competitors, such as Coldwell Banker.

The brand achieved this widespread consumer awareness due to two key factors. First, Century 21 had strong marketplace presence, with offices and agents accessible to all customers. In some trade areas, customers could choose from as many as five or six offices to serve them. Second, Century 21 did an excellent job of using its massive advertising budget, in excess of 100 million dollars per year, to build a strong brand image with a memorable and likable brand personality. The vast majority of the advertising was in the television and newspaper media.

In the late 1980s, Century 21 began experiencing problems. The aggressive expansion of prior years began to show negative effects. While the brand enjoyed high awareness and favorable perceptions among consumers, many of the offices were not delivering the level of quality service expected by customers.

In an aggressive restructuring move, Century 21 designed and implemented new performance and image standards for franchised offices to follow. These included new office signs, new for-sale signage, upgraded gold coats, which were gold-colored business jackets the agents wore that tied in with the company logo colors of brown and gold, and higher quality service performance standards for all offices and agents.

Through franchise terminations and natural attrition, the Century 21 system shrank from 7,500 offices to 5,000 offices. In part, this was positive because the remaining 5,000 offices were more capable of delivering better quality service to customers. This was the intent of the restructuring, the strategy being to further improve customer perceptions of Century 21 to increase customer satisfaction, retention, and repurchase, albeit five or more years down the road. Additionally, this was a key means to generate positive word of mouth, customer referrals, and a boost in the industry.

At the same time this was occurring, the competitive landscape was rapidly shifting. Strong new competitors emerged such as RE/MAX and Prudential. Additionally, the established competition, Coldwell Banker, was growing and becoming a more formidable opponent. Century 21 no longer enjoyed the same market dominance it had in the past.

The restructuring and launch of the new Century 21 image was problematic. There were two problem issues that diluted the brand's image and effectiveness with consumers. The changeover to new signage and gold coats went slowly over the course of a few years, with many offices continuing to use the old signs and coats while others were using the new ones. In many cases, this mixed image occurred within the same market areas. This created a schizophrenic brand personality.

Additionally, with fewer offices, there was now a reduced advertising budget. Previously, not only was the advertising budget larger but the advertising message was focused, crisp, and purposeful in effectively building the Century 21 brand personality.

With the new Century 21 image launch, the advertising strategy departed from the brand's heritage and equity. In attempting to incorporate and communicate the new Century 21 image, the advertising strategy was less clearly defined than in the past. The problem was exacerbated when the company decided to switch advertising agencies in an attempt to recapture the power and magic of previous campaigns. After an exhaustive search of many top advertising agencies, the switch was made from McCann Erikson to Campbell Mithun Esty. With the new agency came all new people who were good advertising professionals yet were lacking experience and understanding of Century 21 and the real estate industry.

The new advertising agency struggled to accurately define an effective advertising strategy. Meanwhile, Century 21 was losing market share. Industry people quipped, "The real estate giant has gone to sleep." In some ways it had. At a time of decreased media expenditures, Century 21 advertising blended in with thousands of messages from other brands competing for the customer's attention. When it was most critical for Century 21 advertising to have a sharper edge to break through the advertising clutter, the advertising went flat.

A new advertising strategy was needed. To accomplish this, management set a new goal, to awaken the sleeping giant by creating new and better marketing and advertising approaches. The first step in the new quest was to re-examine and re-analyze all available customer research, of which there was a lot. The purpose of this exercise was to formulate consumer-based marketing and advertising objectives and strategies. The following is a summary of key highlights from this research.

Research Highlights

For the industry in general, the customer's primary consideration in selecting a real estate company is their perception of the agent of that company. Secondary in importance is the company with which the agent is affiliated. In the customer's mind, it is the real estate agent they are entrusting to successfully guide them through the selling and buying process. Customers feel the real estate selling and buying process is complex and that a well-prepared agent is vital to protecting their interest. The real estate company is important only to the extent it provides resources and tools for the agent to access in the process.

For Century 21, the situation was slightly different. Century 21's strong image and reputation played a more important role in getting the agent to be considered. In many cases, the Century 21 agent was not as well-known or established in the community. Proportionately, Century 21 did not have as many veteran top-producing agents as competitors. Consequently, customers decided to interview Century 21 agents in the selection process on the strength of the company's name. However, once this was accomplished, the agent was evaluated on his or her own strengths.

Most customers will interview and evaluate three different real estate agents before selecting one to sell their home. Most home sellers will buy another home in the same community, thus providing the selling agent two transaction opportunities.

The implication of this research was that the marketing and advertising strategy must focus on the agent. It must effectively communicate reasons why a Century 21 agent is superior to any other. To accomplish this, it is necessary to clearly understand which attributes of an agent are most important in determining the customer's decision.

Research also indicated that there were several important attributes driving a customer's selection of a real estate agent. One attribute was that an agent be professional and knowledgeable. Besides how agents present themselves, this also included their experience, training, and knowledge of the community's schools, shopping, parks, and so forth. Another attribute was that they be committed and hard-working. Clients preferred an agent who would go the extra mile and do whatever it took to get the job done.

Being a good communicator was another attribute. Customers appreciated an agent who would listen and truly understand a customer's needs and wants and one who would stay in touch regularly to keep the customer updated. Being trustworthy and caring was another valued attribute. They wanted an agent who was honest, who could be trusted, and who was easy to relate to, much like relating to a friend. They liked an individual dedicated to the people and community in which they worked.

Customers rated Century 21 agents well in all the attribute categories, but more experienced sellers and buyers gave lower ratings than first-time buyers and sellers. Effective marketing communication would have to focus on further enhancing consumer perceptions of Century 21 agents as possessing these key qualities.

Research showed that 20 percent of all homeowners surveyed expressed a preference for using Century 21 when selling or buying a home. Yet Century 21 had only eight percent of market share. This was an unexplainable discrepancy since customer preference and market share are normally more closely aligned.

Century 21 marketing communications could no longer stop at just building awareness and image, as it had done in the past. To narrow the gap between actual market share and consumer preference, the marketing communications had to do more. They had to work harder to put customers in touch with Century 21 agents more proactively. The passive approach of relying on customers to do the work of finding and contacting agents was no longer effective. With increased competition, the marketing communications had to make it more convenient and attractive for customers to do business with Century 21.

The company took another look at the research implications. Century 21 consumer research results were loaded with impressive data. Customers consistently rated Century 21 as superior to competition in every measure possible. Century 21 was rated as more professional, knowledgeable, trustworthy, better trained, and more capable of getting results. These survey results ranked Century 21 higher on all of these measures by margins ranging from 5 to 1 to as high as 21 to 1.

The conclusions from the research analyses were dependable, primarily because the research was solid. The research results came from extremely well-designed studies with large customer sample sizes. The research studies were validated and re-validated. There was no question that, as underpinnings for a new strategy, these results were as reliable as one could ever expect.

While these research results were impressive, they did nothing to increase market share. However, incorporating them into marketing communications programs would leverage the high rating into increased sales. Based on these research analyses, new objectives and strategies were formulated.

Objectives

The company developed a set of objectives to provide quantifiable benchmarks for an integrated marketing program. These objectives specified that Century 21 would:

- Increase the 8 percent market share to close the gap with customer preference ratings of 20 percent.

- Increase its share of past Century 21 customers' move-up transactions. Of the 250,000 transactions that had occurred five years prior, an estimated 25 percent of these customers would move again in the next year. The sales opportunity was 100,000 potential transactions, including selling the customer's existing home and assisting with the purchase of a new home.

- Increase its share of competitors' past customer move-up transactions. This sales opportunity, estimated at 1,000,000 potential transactions, was a more difficult marketing challenge because these customers may not have had previous experience with Century 21.

- Maintain its share of first-time buyers and stimulate first-time buyer purchases. Historically, Century 21 dominated this customer segment; however, this was a less lucrative segment given that these customers did not have a home to sell and were in a lower price range for a home.

Strategy

The main strategy the company formulated to reach its objectives was to position Century 21 agents as providing the best quality service in the industry, based on three main premises.

- Century 21 agents are more professional, better trained, trustworthy, caring, and hard-working.
- Century 21 agents are rated number one out of ten categories ranked by homeowners.
- With 5,000 offices and 80,000 agents, Century 21 provides its agents with more and better resources to help buyers and sellers.

The desired customer response was: "Century 21 is a name I know and trust. I feel more comfortable that they have the right experience and resources. The Century 21 agent is professional, knowledgeable, caring, and friendly. They have all the things that are important in an agent. I'll call them to find out more."

This strategy was used as a foundation to build a fully integrated marketing communications plan incorporating several key components:

- Television advertising,
- Event sponsorship,
- Direct response media,
- Agent recruiting, and
- World Wide Web.

Television Advertising

Translating the complex new strategy into a company image for a television campaign was a difficult challenge. Several creative options were explored to find the best approach. Two approaches emerged as having the greatest potential. The first featured actual Century 21 agents expressing their thoughts, feelings, and philosophies about quality customer service. The agent's testimonials were mixed with scenes depicting real life situations when the agents were involved with customers during the selling and buying process. The commercial opened and closed with a specially created icon symbolizing the number one ratings customers gave to Century 21 in surveys.

The second approach featured an actual letter from a customer describing how the agent had gone the extra mile in ensuring a successful end result to the real estate transaction. This commercial had a strong emotional edge, exuding warmth and caring and praising the superb quality service.

Both approaches were made into rough commercials on video tape. Drawings, scrap footage from old Century 21 commercials, and other advertisers' commercials were used to make the rough commercials look as realistic as possible.

The test results provided great insight. Both commercial approaches performed very well. The customer letter version was especially effective in communicating the warm, caring, and trustworthy elements. The commercial approach that featured Century 21 agents was stronger in communicating the professional, knowledgeable, well-trained, and hard-working elements of the image.

The rated-number-one icon used in the agent testimonial was very memorable, adding increased credibility to the company and the agents and serving as a powerful summary statement.

The research indicated that both commercial approaches could serve to complement one another and better communicate the campaign strategy. Final modifications and enhancements to each approach incorporated announcer copy and the rated-number-one icon as common elements to tie the approaches together. It was important to ensure that the final execution of the campaign was performed as diligently as the creation of the concepts, which would determine the ultimate success of the campaign.

Several measures were taken to ensure a positive result. First, a massive new search was undertaken to find the best possible customer letter to make into a commercial. The letter used in the research phase was good, but an even better letter would mean an even more effective commercial. Days before the production of the commercial was scheduled to begin, Century 21 received the perfect letter.

The letter was from a new mother in a small town in Indiana. Becky Dilley described how her Century 21 agent had truly gone beyond the call of duty. Mrs. Dilley was not just an ordinary new mother — she had just given birth to sextuplets, four girls and two boys. This was only the second time this had occurred in the United States in the twentieth century. Her agent, Pat, was a truly extraordinary woman. Pat conducted the Dilley home sale process pretty much on her own. While Mrs. Dilley was hospitalized for three months prior to the birth of her sextuplets, Pat did all the legwork in making the Dilley house ready for sale. She also drove 60 miles on a regular basis to visit Mrs. Dilley in the hospital to update her on the progress of the sale. Pat also organized a community diaper drive and collected 10,000 diapers for the Dilly sextuplets. Pat had truly gone well beyond the call of duty. Needless to say, this became the letter that was featured in the commercial. It was a big production, requiring the Dilley family to fly to Hollywood with their six infants so that they could be featured in the commercial.

At the same time, preparation was underway for production of the agent testimonial commercials. Four commercials were planned, two 30-second and two 15-second spots. The plan was to film and edit snippets of agent testimonials from nine different agents. To ensure that the best candidates were used for the commercials, a nation-wide audition session was conducted in which more than 200 Century 21 agents auditioned. The auditions were videotaped and used to select which agents would be flown to Hollywood for filming.

The nine agents were selected because the way they appeared on film truly depicted their real personality and beliefs about what it takes to be an outstanding agent. The resulting lifestyle vignettes were charming, memorable, and relevant.

As a final step of the campaign, both commercials were tested again, and the results were outstanding. The key reason for these commercials achieving high effectiveness scores was the disciplined process followed to choose the right strategy, to use the most effective creative concepts, and to emphasize strong execution.

Effective advertising is a result of following a process such as the one described for Century 21. It does not result merely from the advertising agencies' creative people dreaming up a great advertising idea.

Another key component of the company's improved strategy was a special toll-free telephone number intended to link callers to the closest Century 21 office. This new response mechanism was promoted in all advertising. Setting up this new response mechanism system was a big undertaking, requiring a complex database of all customers and Century 21 offices. The objective was to provide easy and convenient access to the closest Century 21 office by calling 800-4-HOUSES and entering the customer's zip code. This would transfer the call immediately to the closest office. It provided convenience to the customer and gave the offices and agents a unique advantage in the marketplace. When they went on appointments with prospective clients, agents could use this new technology as an example of Century 21's superior capabilities in selling homes.

Event Sponsorship

To lessen the impact of its reduced media budget, Century 21 had to revamp its media strategy. It did this by decreasing its length of commercials and increasing its use of event sponsorship.

Shorter commercials were used for the first time to increase media coverage. The new 15-second spots worked extremely well, communicating the strategy effectively. The greater use of 15-second spots increased Century 21 advertising exposure by 50 percent.

The second significant strategy shift was increased use of high-impact event programming. Three or four times a year, Century 21 sponsored programs such as the major league baseball all-star game and the Olympics. These programs provided greater visibility to consumers as well as to the franchisees and agents. Including franchisees and agents as part of the target audience became an important matter because they had expressed dissatisfaction with the companies' advertising program. The key advantage Century 21 was expected to provide was its powerful advertising support and instant customer awareness. Thus it was critical to re-establish their confidence that the advertising program was providing them this support.

Event sponsorships also provided opportunities for special promotions. These included contests that awarded free trips to the Olympics, along with agent brochures that promoted the event sponsorship to potential sellers as another demonstration of Century 21's power in reaching potential buyers.

In the case of the Olympic sponsorship, this was a unique opportunity to tie in the new Century 21 rated-number-one icon with the Olympic theme. Posters and brochures were created that featured the new gold icon along with the Olympic rings and the headline "Century 21 is bringing home the Gold."

In another key media strategy shift, the company set up a reserve fund for last-minute opportunistic purchases of programs. By letting the television networks know of their interest in these advertising opportunities, Century 21 became the first company contacted when one of these situations opened. Some examples of programming purchased this way were the basketball playoff games and the baseball World Series. Commercials in these programs were purchased at twenty to thirty percent below the market rate.

Direct Response Media

The direct response part of the Century 21 marketing program had two objectives. The first was to convert potential customers with a predisposition to use Century 21 into actual customers. The second objective was to reach real estate agents to persuade them to affiliate with Century 21. Three key components of the Century 21 direct response marketing program focused on an infomercial campaign, direct mail and direct response print targeted to buyers and sellers, and direct response advertising targeted to recruit new real estate agents.

The infomercial campaign was based on the same strategy as the national brand image TV campaign. However, instead of a 30-second communication, there were 30 minutes to convey a more complete message and to generate qualified leads.

The infomercial featured top Century 21 agents providing helpful advice to educate and inform consumers. Portraying the Century 21 agents as helpful, professional, and knowledgeable enhanced the overall Century 21 brand image. Additionally at strategic points in the infomercial, the agents would discuss particular real estate services especially important to consumers. The agents would subtly communicate that Century 21 possessed these resources. Some of the topics that fell into this category were how to obtain the right financing, how to inexpensively prepare the appearance of a home to make it more salable, and how to go about selecting the right real estate agent.

The agent interview segments were interspersed with entertaining re-enactments of several customer letters received by Century 21. The four letters selected covered a cross section of buyers and sellers. Each letter told about the outstanding quality service provided by a Century 21 agent. For example, one letter described how an agent went beyond the call of duty to help a retiring U.S. Air Force colonel and his family to sell their home and buy another while the family was stationed overseas. Another letter was from a recently widowed senior citizen who told how caring and sensitive the Century 21 agent had been in helping her to sell the family home.

When the two distinct parts were edited together, the infomercial was very effective in enhancing the Century 21 brand image. The agent segments demonstrated professionalism, knowledge, and resources. The letters demonstrated customer validation that Century 21 agents were hard-working, caring, and results-oriented. Together, the two film approaches told the entire Century 21 story.

Relevant promotional offers were strategically placed throughout the infomercial. One offer was for a set of real estate guide books free to those who called an 800 number. The caller's name, address, phone number, and purchasing or selling intentions were collected and forwarded to the closest Century 21 office for follow-up. The offices were instructed to have an agent deliver the free guidebooks to people who responded to the offer.

The direct mail program focused on three main customer types: past customers, first-time buyers, and empty-nesters.

Past Century 21 customers, designated as members of the Century 21 Preferred Client Club, received a glossy bi-monthly newsletter produced by Century 21. The newsletter, filled with helpful information geared to homeowners, provided a way to maintain a relationship with the customer for future business and referrals.

These same past customers received a series of targeted direct mail communications timed for when the customer had lived in their home for five or more years. This strategy was based on research which indicated many homeowners were in the market for a new home at the five-year point. The direct mail communication had a message tailored to these customers of "Trust us again to sell your home and find you another." It also had information about monthly payments based on current interest rates to make the point that in many cases the customer's buying power was greater than it had been when they purchased their existing home. The direct mailer also included a promotional offer especially appealing to this customer segment, a sweepstakes offer to win free mortgage payments for a year.

First-time buyers were also targeted, first by compiling a list of names of potential buyers, for example people who were currently renters, earning over $35,000 per year, and recently married or having a child. These potential customers were sent a direct mail communication centered around the proposition of "Let us show you how you can own your own home for no more than what you are currently paying in rent." The mailers also included a promotional offer of a sweepstakes to win a $21,000 down payment.

The third target segment was empty-nesters, homeowners over the age of 55 with children living outside of the family home. The customized communication to them was "Let us show you how to cash out of that too-large home and invest in your retirement." The accompanying promotional offer was a sweepstakes to win free air travel for a year.

In each case, the custom tailored direct mail communication included information about Century 21's unique qualifications to assist the customer with their particular real estate needs. The sales promotion components included in each mailer were designed to stimulate interest and generate qualified customer leads through an 800 number and business reply cards.

Another aspect of the direct response program was to use select magazine and newspaper publications to reach very specialized markets. This might include investors interested in real estate as an investment option who could be reached through the *Wall Street Journal*. Customers with a potential interest in a second home were reached through lifestyle and recreation magazines such as *Travel and Leisure*, *Golf Digest*, and skiing magazines.

Agent Recruiting

Increasing the agent population was critical in order to more effectively grow market share. Two main methods were used to recruit qualified agents for Century 21 offices.

For existing experienced agents who currently worked for competitors, the company placed ads in real estate trade magazines. These ads featured top Century 21 agents discussing the secrets of their success and how the Century 21 system contributed to this success. In addition, a series of direct mail pieces were sent to top producing agents of competitive companies. Designed to be highly attention getting, these mailers portrayed Century 21 as the undisputed leader in real estate.

A separate campaign was designed to reach qualified individuals in non-real estate industries and communicate the unique benefits of a career with Century 21. Key potential agent segments included customer service professionals, nurses, teachers, retired military officers, and managers in companies that were downsizing. To reach these people, Century 21 used television commercials scheduled in news-oriented programming such as CNN, custom-tailored magazine ads, and direct mail with messages uniquely suited to each of the targeted groups. In each case, successful Century 21 agents, who had similar career backgrounds as the targeted potential agent, were used to convey the message of how the agent's experience and skills, acquired prior to real estate, prepared them for a successful career as a Century 21 agent.

In each of these custom-tailored advertising programs, the imagery was consistent with all Century 21 advertising to establish the same brand image in consumers minds.

World Wide Web

A Century 21 Web site was created to provide information and further build customers' preferences to use the Century 21 system. The Web site contained information specifically geared towards the four areas of home buying, home selling, listings of homes, and career opportunities.

For buyers, the Web site noted important things to understand and look for in buying a home. In addition there were interactive programs that allowed buyers to determine the price of home they could qualify for. Furthermore, information was provided for a wide range of mortgage programs with interest rate, monthly payment information, and explanations on the benefits and appropriateness of each mortgage program.

For sellers, it gave tips for fixing up and preparing their home for sale as well as information and criteria to use in selecting a real estate agent.

For home listings, a variety of homes for sale were included in the Web site so that customers were able to review price and features of homes for sale in all parts of the country.

Given the importance of recruiting new agents, the Web site included information about career opportunities in real estate in general and for Century 21 in particular.

Century 21 was successful in improving sales trends by applying integrated marketing principles. The starting point, or foundation, was a thorough review of the research. This lead to defining specific measurable objectives and designing a multi-faceted marketing communications program. The process required a rigorous study of all possible marketing tactics and creativity and imagination in deployment of each tactic.

Automotive Case Study

This automotive dealership case study demonstrates how a combination of database development, direct mail, inbound and outbound telemarketing, sales promotion, and Internet marketing communication tactics can improve brand marketing effectiveness.

Vehicle Sales

The process of retaining existing customers, reactivating past customers, and acquiring new customers is far more effective with direct response marketing communication techniques in support of the brand's mass media program. Here again, the process of creating personalized communication programs which specifically address individual customer needs and wants leads to greater response and return on marketing investment. An effectively designed marketing program can positively impact all four of the factors which determine customer satisfaction, loyalty, and purchase.

The number one factor affecting loyalty is a customer's previous ownership of a vehicle. Naturally, there are many things that will effect ownership experience which are out of the realm of marketing communication. But experience has shown that ongoing marketing communication can influence a customer's perceived satisfaction and loyalty. This is accomplished through establishing a dialogue with customers which makes them feel special and cared for. Dialogue is increased when a company provides an 800 number, e-mail address, or mailing address through which customers can give their input on a range of relevant subjects.

The second most important element is the test drive. Marketing cannot effect the actual test drive experience, but it can affect how many prospective buyers actually take a test drive. Test drive frequency can be increased with carefully established incentives.

A third important component of perceived satisfaction is how the customer is treated after the sale. Many salespeople are not good at staying in touch with customers. With ongoing communication sent on the salesperson's behalf, the customer does not feel abandoned by their salesperson.

The fourth factor, advice from friends and family, is not totally within the reach of marketing and advertising. However, this key element in the purchase decision can serve as an advantage to the auto dealer. Positive word-of-mouth advertising is generated by establishing a program which encourages satisfied owners to actively communicate their satisfaction to friends and family.

All good marketing programs start with carefully defined objectives and goals. Here are the objectives chosen by the automotive dealer.

- Boost new vehicle sales.
- Increase repurchases.
- Increase dealership traffic.
- Generate referrals.
- Develop leads for first-time buyers.
- Support long-term customer relationships.
- Promote advocacy among current owners.
- Educate dealers about the importance of owner satisfaction to long-term success.

The process of building relationships, loyalty, and advocacy encompasses the entire period the customer owns the vehicle. Consequently, it is critical to recognize the importance of vehicle maintenance and repair during the entire ownership period. Effective relationship building, loyalty, and advocacy processes are really a collective and fully integrated marketing program, which should include all marketing communication to the customer for repair and maintenance. For the purposes of this case study, however, vehicle purchase and maintenance and repair are separate marketing discussions.

Use Marketing to Build Customer Relationships

The ideal time to reinforce the purchase decision and begin to build customer loyalty and advocacy is just after the vehicle purchase decision has been made. The following are strategies for the first marketing communication to a recent buyer.

Special Thank You — First-time Buyers

A special thank you sent to first-time buyers should accomplish these goals:

- Introduce the dealer's service facilities.
- Reinforce their purchase decisions.
- Provide an item relevant to vehicle satisfaction which serves as a lasting reminder of loyalty and prompts inquiries from friends and relatives.
- Encourage the owner to make referrals, either through a simple, "Tell your friends and neighbors" or a formal referral program.

The communication should include certain points.

- A gesture of appreciation,
- Information which reinforces the decision to buy the vehicle, such as satisfaction survey results,
- A lasting token for the car or home, such as a rolodex card or refrigerator magnet with the dealer name, addressee, and phone numbers, and
- An incentive to use the dealership for maintenance and repairs, such as coupon offers of a free or reduced-price oil change for their first service. This is important because research has shown that up to 40 percent of newer vehicle owners never or rarely use the dealership for service. An early incentive can help direct service behavior toward the dealership, which provides an opportunity for more dealership contact and customer satisfaction.

Another tactic which should be used whenever possible is a personalized letter from the dealer stating that, "Your sales associate, John Doe, felt you should have the gift enclosed because of your valued loyalty." The dealer can custom-tailor the creative package to promote service hours, shuttle service, loaners, or other benefits.

The marketing communications message should be further customized to first-time buyers, male and females, couples with children, and so forth, so that it is as relevant and personal as possible to that customer.

Special Thank You — Repeat Owners

A special thank you sent to repeat owners could be fundamentally the same communication as the first-time owner piece, with certain modifications so that it includes:

- Acknowledgment and thank-you for the repeat business and continued loyalty,
- An offer of a free gift at the dealer's expense, and
- A gold or platinum status designation to differentiate it from the first-time buyer letter.

All communications should identify the local dealer, the salesperson whenever possible, and the corporation as the source of the communication so that the relationship develops between the customer, the local dealer, and the brand.

It should also include flexible components such as offers which the dealer can custom-tailor to best meet local needs. This also allows the dealer to address particular market situations and to have involvement, or buy-in, with the program.

Referral Programs

A referral program should motivate satisfied customers to refer friends and relatives for dealer visits and test drives. The referral mechanism used should be relevant to your brand and easy for the customer to use.

Available options should be pre-tested to select those most effective. The following is an example of one interactive incentive program with concepts that can be included within a simple one-piece mailer or expanded to a more elaborate two-piece mailing.

Package One

The first mail piece would include a key chain as a free gift. It would also include a letter that thanks the owner for their loyalty, includes facts to reinforce their purchase decision, and introduces the referral program, or just includes a teaser such as "Stay tuned for Part Two."

Package Two

The second mail piece would include five or more reproductions of automobile keys which serve as referral mechanisms that the vehicle owner could give to friends and relatives to generate referral lead traffic to the dealer's showroom. Each key would be imprinted with the vehicle owner's ID number. The mail piece would explain that, when a person brings a key to the dealer, both owner and prospect will be automatically entered into a sweepstakes. Depending on cost considerations, the grand prize could be a new vehicle. Additional prizes should include items such as accessories or free service.

Besides offering the referral program to new owners, it could be offered twice each year to those owners who actively participated in the program in the past. Also, send referral offers to internal employees at the corporate, regional, and local dealer levels as well. Employee sweepstakes entries would be in a separate pool.

Use names from the referral sweepstakes entries to create a database for later communications. You want to maintain contact with those individuals who have expressed an interest in purchasing a vehicle but are delaying an actual purchase. This will increase the chances of them purchasing from you when they do act.

Repurchase Program

A repurchase program should focus on communicating prime vehicle and brand features, benefits, support, and incentives in order to influence future purchase decisions. Again, you should pre-test a variety of incentives to determine the most cost-effective ones. Here is a list of various incentive ideas to stimulate your own brain storming.

- One share of company stock, framed
- Monetary contribution to M.A.D.D. (Mothers Against Drunk Drivers)
- Free visor organizer
- Poster of vehicle with owner's name on license plate
- 10 percent off all emergency repairs
- Free or discounted roadside assistance program
- Preferred lease program
- Preferred auto insurance package for owner
- Cash refund of $250, $500, $750, or more
- Discounts on accessories and extended warranty programs
- Free upgrade package for leather upholstery or air conditioning
- Free road atlas

To assure the most effective approach, test various incentives with different segments of neutral and satisfied owners. Then use some predictive methods to determine each customer's likelihood to respond. Next, choose the most cost-effective incentives to include in your mailing. Different segments of these owners would receive different value incentives, based on predicted response.

Continually research and test the most promising alternative strategies and tactics. For example, if a cash refund of $1,000 is effective, then test a refund offer of $750 to better determine the optimal return on investment. Through statistical analysis you may discover that customer segments can be motivated to purchase using lower refund offers.

Direct Mail Program

Newsletters, with parts and service information or referral program details, could be customized by the dealer. One section could open a dialogue with customers to determine their needs and wants. It would include response mechanisms such as 800 numbers, reply cards, and e-mail addresses.

Vary the creative message according to a customer's needs and wants, interests and motivations. For example, variations may be based on safety, style, speed and handling, price, comfort, or leasing options.

Parts and Service Programs

Parts and service programs are very important to an automotive dealer's marketing strategy. Contacting owners in regard to a vehicle's ongoing maintenance is the dealer's primary means of increasing brand loyalty and the likelihood of repurchase. The quality of the service that an owner actually receives at the dealership will outweigh the impact of marketing. However, assuming that the service experience is good, a well-designed direct mail program can have a significant impact on a customer's perceived satisfaction with their vehicle and dealer.

Studies have shown that a minimum of nine customer contacts or communications per year are necessary to positively affect customer loyalty. The best means of reaching this frequency level is through service marketing. This can include service reminders and promotional mailers which a customer may receive from a dealer.

Given the importance of service programs, the following facts and their implications will give you an in-depth look at what research reveals about this market.

The foundation of a successful program lies in a thorough understanding of the potential market. This includes 1) examining the service marketplace, 2) identifying the priorities of the service managers in order to provide a program that will both support them and tap their knowledge of what they feel owners want, 3) identifying owners' wants and needs to increase customer response, and 4) comparing dealer service prices with competitors' prices.

Nationwide, there are more than 350,000 automobile service outlets and, at most, only a few thousand dealers for a given make and usually far fewer. In total, service providers spend hundreds of millions of dollars annually to advertise their services to consumers while dealers spend far less. The implication is that consumers are more likely to think of and consider using a service provider, rather than a dealer, for many of their service visits.

To compete with this vast competition, dealers need to develop a highly effective service marketing program integrated with their new vehicle advertising campaigns so that both sales and service can capitalize on the efforts of each other.

Consumers are keeping autos longer and driving more miles per year on average, thus increasing their automobile service needs. Dealers are generally the first choice for most services during the first year of ownership. After that, however, owners use competitive service providers for many of their services.

The chart below compares the percent of consumers choosing the dealer versus other providers after the first year.

Professional Installation Service by Outlet
(percent of consumers choosing)

Type of Work Performed	New Car Dealer	Other
Brake	17.9	82.1
Carburetor and fuel	49.0	51.0
Cooling	17.0	83.0
Electrical	18.1	81.9
Engine	29.6	70.4
Exhaust	6.8	93.2
Oil	21.8	78.2
Shocks and struts	8.6	91.4
Alignment and chassis	19.0	81.0
Transmission	26.8	73.2
Tune-up	29.3	70.7

In a national study, consumers rated the factors that determine their choice for automotive service in the following order:

1. Quality of work
2. Convenience
3. Quality customer service
4. Price

The factors weighing most heavily in a customer's choice of service outlet, as shown in the chart on the next page, indicate that quality of service is the top factor and type of brand sold the least important factor.

Factors Influencing Where Consumers Have Service Performed			
Quality of work	37.8%	Price	12.8%
Convenience	24.9%	Product breadth	6.2%
Service	13.7%	Brands sold	4.6%

Service preference and usage vary by region of the country. For example, consumers in the northeastern United States use gas stations and repair garages to a greater extent for a tune-up. People in east central states are more likely to use dealerships, and consumers on the west coast are more likely to use a tune-up specialist.

Factor	Region
All users of tune-up	N.S.*
Do-it yourselfers	N.S.*
Relative or friend	South
Gas station	Northeast
Repair garage	Northeast
New car dealership	East central
Tune-up specialist	Pacific

* N.S. means factor is not significant.

The implication is that, although consumers use the dealer for most service the first year, they somehow get out of the habit afterward. This is probably due to the consumer tiring of the less convenient locations of dealers and succumbing to the heavy advertising pressure and market presence of the other service providers.

Clearly, dealers must grab the opportunity to develop programs which maintain the pattern of customers using their dealership beyond the first year after purchase.

In all regions, the opportunity exists to create a stronger personal relationship between dealer and consumer which can compete with the personal relationship and convenience of the local service station.

While price was ranked fourth in importance, if the consumer perceives a large price discrepancy between alternative service providers, it becomes a critical barrier. Consumer research has indicated that the perceived price gap between the dealer and other providers is quite wide. This becomes a key reason for developing communication messages and coupon offers to change this perception.

More consumer research results continue to become available, with new factors for you to consider. For example, a survey was mailed to 1,500 randomly-selected vehicle owners to identify service usage behavior, what factors such as price or convenience most influence their choices, and their ratings for a range of coupon offers. The following results summarize the nearly 650 responses received.

Consumers want service offers they need and use frequently, such as an oil change. It stands to reason that an effective array of coupon offers in a mailing should include as many frequently used services as possible.

Special promotional offers most likely to convince people to take their vehicle to the dealership for service were:

- $9.95 oil and lube,
- Free transmission inspection,
- Free loaner car,
- Buy-one-get-one-free oil change for $19.95,
- 24-point inspection for $1.99,
- 10 percent credit toward future service or new car purchase, and
- Discounted vouchers for packages of services.

The results also revealed these points:

- Promoting the factory technician's knowledge and expertise was meaningful and helpful in reinforcing the benefits of a dealer.
- Brand name parts were perceived as an advantage for using a dealer.
- Consumers preferred simple, brief, easily-understood notices and mailers.
- Coupon offers should clearly communicate the discounted price, original price, savings, and service offered, with no strings attached.
- Consumers responded positively to the idea of local competitive price information included in the mailers.

- Consumers liked dealer newsletters but only if they contained useful, factual, and helpful information.

- Consumers preferred a greater number of coupons in the mailers because there would be a greater likelihood of one or more fitting their needs.

An opportunity exists to leverage the perceived strengths which dealers provide for original parts and quality service. An additional opportunity exists for convincing owners of the benefits the dealer offers over competitors for services such as brakes, exhaust, and transmission work. The focus should be on the benefits of the technicians' superior training and knowledgeability of a specific vehicle make. By frequently communicating these benefits, dealers can be more successful in performing a greater share of all service repairs.

The dealer has an ideal opportunity to promote these competitive prices through direct mail programs specifically by having local price surveys as part of the coupon mailers. The chart below is an example of a price comparison that could be mailed to customers.

Competitive Pricing Comparison

	Oil Change/ Filter	Tire Rotation/ Balance	Minor Service	Major Service	Radiator Flush/Fill	Align- ment
Dealer	$22.25	$43.40	$43.89	$176.80	$50.40	$59.59
Goodyear	19.35	39.00	59.99	167.00	42.80	54.99
Firestone	18.09	36.00	49.99	164.00	54.00	60.00
Pep Boys	21.99	42.00	47.99	206.00	50.18	51.99
Local independent	23.96	34.40	69.39	177.00	42.80	74.50

Dealer prices on these key services are competitive in all cases, far more competitive than consumer perceptions have indicated in research.

The automotive dealer's service managers can provide a wealth of information for successful marketing. The attitudes and needs of these service managers provide the second aspect of market information necessary for designing the most effective marketing programs.

The facts are that significant opportunities exist for dealers to capture a greater share of service revenue. However, competition has proliferated and made great strides in marketplace presence and advertising impressions. These advantages often outweigh consumers' preference to use a dealer for service.

The facts also indicate that dealer service managers have expressed frustration with many of factory-administered marketing programs because of high cost, standardization without attention to regional differences, and mailing list over-segmentation. Dealers also feel the factory programs' creative packages lack variety and have poor timing and inadequate frequency of mailings. Consequently, dealers must develop and implement their own marketing program to supplement the factory program. Yet, these programs can often be expensive and difficult to manage and execute. Additionally, the brand image projected by these efforts may not be consistent with the brand image the corporation has spent vast resources to create.

The implications of this are that dealers want a centrally-developed, cost-effective program which allows flexibility and creative package alternatives to more effectively supplement the factory mail program. Importantly, the brand image projected in a centrally-administered program would be controlled and consistent with the image of the national media campaign.

Research findings among more than 255 service managers nationwide did validate much existing knowledge, yet some new insights were revealed. The majority of service managers feel that coupon mailers are effective but believe they are more effective with current customers than prospects.

	Effective/ Very Effective
Effectiveness of coupon mailers	67%
Effectiveness of coupon mailers to existing customers	80%
Effectiveness of coupon mailing to prospects	40%

Many service managers favor sending both service reminders and coupon mailers to existing customers because they see better results among this group. Additionally, this more frequent mail contact and coupon promotion can help retain existing customers.

However, several opportunities exist here for those who are enterprising enough to seek further results. One challenge would be to improve the effectiveness of coupon mailers to customer prospects. Or a dealer could educate service managers on the need and role of coupon offers in generating revenue they may not have otherwise had. There is also an opportunity to refine the coupon mailers sent to existing customers to make them even more profitable, such as, for example, by promoting those services for which these customers do not usually use the dealership.

A key portion of the study focused on identifying the most important features of a service and parts direct mail program. Both existing knowledge and new insights are noted.

	Validated Existing Knowledge	New Insight
More frequent mail intervals	X	
More coupons, more "build own"	X	
Want to know their input is valued and used	X	
Make sure the list is accurate and up-to-date	X	
Availability of regular results tracking	X	
More creative formats		✓
Want advice and guidance on what works		✓
Programs which let them better target customer and prospects by sending different types of messages to current customers versus prospects		✓
To be able to identify when a vehicle is likely to need major repairs, based on reasonable actual miles on vehicle, etc.		✓

The survey research also revealed respondent opinions through answers to open-ended questions. These are some of the responses.

- "The disadvantage of all the programs in California is the lack of accurate mailing lists for prospective customers."

- "I would like to have a variety of formats."
- "Some tracking results appear to be, and in some cases have proven to be, inaccurate or over-inflated."
- "Weakness — factory program goes out quarterly. Other than that, it's great."
- "Weakness — timely mailings."
- "There seems to be a lack of creativity in the advertising field. Everyone comes out with these examples and says which design do you like, and we can customize your coupons. I tried out the same old coupon month after month. No one seems to care about an advertisement."
- "Too much lead time (five months) required."
- "Impersonal, not colorful, nor are they creative."
- "No pizzazz — bland, middle-of-the-road graphics."
- "Mailer is not personalized enough to promote dealer image."
- "Follow up with customers who do not respond to mailers to find out why."
- "Would like various styles of artwork for both reminders and coupons."

The implication here is that it is very important to build a marketing program with suggestions from service managers in order to allow them to have more ownership of the program. Such suggestions are that you:

- Vary the formats.
- Improve the accuracy of mailing lists.
- Include more coupons and more build-your-own offer packages.
- Have a follow-up program and solid marketing guidance on ways to improve programs.
- Vary the coupon mailers sent to existing customers and prospects, with prospects receiving more aggressive coupon offers and existing customers receiving less aggressive coupon offers.
- Offer custom-tailored programs to customers expected to need major repairs, such as transmission, shocks, water pump, and alternator work. Identify these customer groups based on reasonable expectancies of various repairs and on age and mileage of vehicles.

Managers felt favorably towards direct mailers, which they ranked in order of perceived effectiveness in this way.

Type	Rank
Envelope package	1
Self-mailer	2
Newsletter	3
Postcard	4

With all these research facts at your fingertips, it is now time to apply them in ways that will make your business more successful. Start by formulating objectives. The automotive dealer decided it could profitably build parts and service market share by successfully accomplishing these objectives:

- Maintain service visit frequency for loyal users and increase frequency among semi-loyal users.
- Build dealer and factory profit margins by offering discounts on selected parts and service, based on consumer usage patterns.
- Expand the scope of the average service visit, to provide greater convenience to the customer and more revenue to the dealer.
- Allow dealers to compete more effectively by providing them greater flexibility and support in developing local marketing programs.

When objectives are set, decide on some strategies that will help achieve those objectives. The automotive research led to very good brand positioning strategies, which were to:

- Maintain current loyal customers, increase usage of semi-loyal customers, and stimulate trial and retrial among non-users; and
- Achieve increased satisfaction among all owners and repurchase by current in-market owners.

The idea was to promote the dealer as a superior maintenance and repair service value. The dealer could now specify the reasons why the service was superior. The dealer had:

- Factory-trained technicians with superior knowledge of the vehicle make,
- One-stop convenience for all service needs,
- Transportation provided for convenience,

- Valuable service specials in addition to competitive everyday pricing, and
- Genuine brand name parts.

At this point, brand image becomes an important factor in marketing strategy. Brand image means that you want the brand and the dealer to be known as knowledgeable, trustworthy, fair, and quality-oriented, as a specialist of your vehicle's make who understands your needs and is always willing to provide help and assistance.

The desired customer perception was: "The dealer is more reasonably priced than I thought, and I can trust them because they know my vehicle better. It is easier to use the dealership because they can do everything needed for my vehicle, and I don't have to shop around."

To get the greatest return on your marketing investment, use this positioning strategy with custom-tailored communication tactics to establish a dialogue with different customer types.

There are several applications of customized marketing for parts and service. At the most basic level are coupon mailers with meaningful and relevant messages to customers and prospects. Personalize the marketing communication to address these owners' unique needs and motivations. This is a starting point to begin identifying additional ways to expand the program to different owners.

Information to help you start developing one-to-one marketing programs in many cases already exists. For example, you could start with a thorough analysis of the repair orders currently collected. This would provide data pinpointing owner service behavior from which you could determine: 1) the extent to which they use the dealership for service, 2) how valuable the customer is in terms of dollars spent, 3) customers who have used the dealership previously but not within the past 6 to 12 months, and 4) types of services they use the dealership for and those they do not.

This data would also be an important starting point to predict when a vehicle is likely to need certain major repairs and thus allow you to develop timed, pre-emptive communication to these owners. Other data to use in defining potential marketing approaches includes vehicle model type, under warranty, lease, new or used vehicle owners, non-responders to coupon offers, mail or telephone responsive, and proximity to dealer.

Customers who own older vehicles are a specific group to target for parts and service sales. Many service managers do not feel it is productive to market to owners of older models, the rationale being that response rate is lower and that technicians prefer to work on newer models to practice their latest, state-of-the-art training. However, older vehicles generally require more repairs and more parts and so provide more revenue than newer models. With even a small response rate, these vehicles should provide a substantial return on investment.

Providing incentives to service managers for marketing to older vehicles is effective. Some incentives to consider are to:

- Provide higher corporate subsidies for mailers targeted to older models.
- Increase parts rebates for older vehicles.
- Reward and recognize technicians who perform the less glamorous repair jobs required by older models.

Another effective marketing strategy is a pre-emptive value offer, which is a highly discounted price on an everyday basis with no coupon requirement.

Considering experience and research, much is accomplished by designing a strong marketing strategy that states that repair services at a dealer are a good value. Two sets of data support this. First was the unjustified perception among consumers that the dealer is much more expensive. Secondly, research showed that customers prefer not to wait for and collect coupons for service, that it is a hassle for them.

This leads to possible strategic approaches where one or more key service items are priced aggressively lower than competition and promoted as everyday values, with no coupon necessary. Here you could use both direct mail advertising and point-of-purchase merchandising. It would not take a significant price decrease to accomplish this, and the increased customer traffic, loyalty, and add-on services it would generate should more than offset lower margins on the service items being promoted.

The everyday values featured in this strategy would be oil changes performed every 3,000 miles and tire rotation performed every 5,000 miles. Additionally, a part of the package could feature a 24-point vehicle inspection for $1.99. This would serve both to further enhance value perceptions and to provide opportunities to perform additional services.

Telemarketing was another strategy used. Research among service managers revealed certain trends regarding the use of telemarketing to encourage customers to come in for service.

- 40 percent use telemarketing.
- 80 percent of these use telemarketing as a reminder of when service is due.
- Of those who use telemarketing, most felt it was effective.

An important factor of the telemarketing approach is to keep the call brief. The brevity is what allows the expense of this medium to be cost-effective and practical as a marketing tool. The tone of the call should be service-oriented, reminding the customer of the service due and offering to set a convenient time for an appointment.

In addition, four or five closed-end questions are included to identify service motivation among the customers contacted. Questions identifying whether the service was performed somewhere else or the vehicle was disposed of are included. You might structure the survey questions as shown below.

This survey approach also serves as a softer sell in actually setting appointments. The questions should focus on price, quality work, convenience, and trust.

Customers' answers provide data to explain and correlate actual behavior, such as why customers returned or did not return to the dealership. Many variables, such as vehicle model, owner's age and sex, can be analyzed. You may determine exactly what some owners respond to, be it price, convenience, telephone reminders or mail reminders, for example.

The Role of Sales Promotion

Sales promotion can be a very effective component in an ongoing marketing communication program to increase customer interest and provide added value for the customer. These are some examples of sales promotion tactics to consider incorporating into your program.

- Have a special preferred customer program. Some of the benefits could be a) a free key chain as an in-car service reminder, b) a sweepstakes offer for a new vehicle entered by scanning the bar coded key chain at the cashier area of the service department, c) 10 percent off all emergency repairs, and d) free car wash. The dealership can select which benefits to offer at what time.

- Add a sweepstakes entry to the coupon portions of mailings to increase consumer response and capture more data.

- Use a standard, everyday offer of a free 12 or 24-point safety inspection each time a vehicle is serviced at a participating dealership. This should be visibly promoted at the dealership and in all mailings. To the consumer, this offer adds value and provides a competitive superiority for the dealer by helping to ensure their safety and convenience by detecting possible problems that are correctable at that visit. This is an opportunity to educate consumers that comprehensive troubleshooting is an advantage a dealer can provide that gives the dealer a competitive advantage. For the dealer, it provides a management tool to assure the service department has a consistent, disciplined, and proactive system for expanding the scope of the average service visit and maximizing revenue potential.

- Provide a free current model loaner car while the owner's car is being serviced for a select group of customers or for owners who are ready for a new car purchase.

The chart on the next page rates various promotional offers that were identified in consumer research as having strong potential in getting vehicle owners to use the dealership more often for service. Taken from 650 customer responses nationwide, the data is categorized by customers who use a dealership for service occasionally/sometimes, often/always, and never/rarely. Percentages indicate to what degree each type of customer would be likely to use a dealership for service because of that particular promotional offer. A mean rating is also included for each concept, based on a scale of 1 to 4 (1:4), with 1 being much more likely to use the dealership and 4 being not likely to use the dealership.

Customer Ratings of Likely Response to Dealership Offers

Special Offers	Customer Use of Dealer Service			Total	Mean
	Never/ Rarely	Occasionally/ Sometimes	Often/ Always		
Free loaner car	52%	57%	64%	59%	1.6
$9.95 oil and lube	48	62	65	60	1.6
Buy-one-get-one-free oil change	33	52	68	55	1.7
Free transmission inspection	42	61	60	56	1.7
Free brake inspection and minor brake repair	38	30	52	43	1.8
$1.99 24-point inspection	38	47	58	49	1.8
10% credit for purchase of new vehicle or future repair	45	30	60	48	1.9
Discounted maintenance and repair vouchers	26	46	52	44	1.9
Extended drop-off and pick-up hours	23	41	51	41	1.9
Preferred customer club	26	42	48	41	1.9
$48 tune-up special	29	40	45	39	2.0
$59 front or rear brake special	27	23	38	31	2.1
Special discounts based on dollar amount spent	32	26	38	33	2.1
All parts guaranteed 12 months or 12,000 miles	21	26	40	31	2.2
10% discount on auto insurance	36	30	41	37	2.2
$19.95 oil and lube in 30 minutes or less	32	23	33	30	2.2
$59 transmission service special	23	23	37	29	2.2
Winning prizes when visiting dealer	43	13	31	29	2.3
Loan of up to $2,000 for repairs at dealership	22	31	41	33	2.3
Transportation when car is dropped off for service	15	21	41	29	2.3
$45 cooling system special	14	17	6	20	2.4
Receiving a catalog of accessories from dealer	15	26	29	25	2.4

Service Reminder Programs

Based on research, the key things that service managers want in service reminder programs are:

- Reminders which can be sent using third class postage,
- A variety of creative formats,
- Dealer identification on outside of mailings, and
- The ability to include dealer-specific information.

An effective service reminder program should address these needs and include two other features.

Service reminders should be completely integrated with the overall parts and service marketing program. Repair order data which is collected from each of the dealerships should be added to the primary database to enhance your knowledge and understanding of owners' service behavior. This allows you to define current customers versus prospects at the most basic level. The repair order data also provides information such as frequency of dealer visits, degree of loyalty, and services purchased outside of the dealership.

Dealer-funded telemarketing follow-up services should be offered to dealers. Service managers have the best intentions of conducting their own telephone follow-up program; however, due to time and resource constraints, they generally do not have a professional, consistent system in place.

The ideal service reminder program would also 1) access dealership repair order data at least weekly, 2) use vehicle mileage information to process timely service reminder mailers weekly, and 3) after sending a reminder, follow up with a telephone call to those owners who have not responded to the reminder within two weeks of its delivery. A program which offers these three key features will maximize the number of customer service visits and your return on investment.

The combination of one letter and a follow-up telephone call eliminates the repetition of multiple letters. It also provides a proactive way to immediately set an appointment on the telephone with the customer. Importantly, it allows you to identify if and why a customer does not intend to respond to the reminder. It provides first-hand information about dissatisfied customers, what competitors they may be using, and whether they have sold or disposed of their vehicle. This can reveal key information to develop more effective service and marketing programs.

Execution is absolutely critical to making the right strategy or program truly effective. The best program in the world will fail unless individuals responsible for implementation understand it, believe in it, and use it. This requires a multi-faceted communication process which includes personal contact at every level within the organization. You will need to plan for the complexity and difficulty in achieving understanding, buy-in, and use of any program.

Ideas for ensuring proper understanding and effective use of programs include conducting half-day marketing seminars throughout the year for dealership managers and sales personnel. You can also initiate and conduct in-person, in-depth consultations with dealership managers. Every manager should receive at least one consult per year, with a priority list of managers receiving two to four consultations a year. These efforts should increase buy-in and use of a program, but repeating these key steps will be necessary to achieve long-term success.

Tracking and Analysis

Tracking and analysis of a direct marketing program's effectiveness is the foundation for improving and enhancing the program and moving it to the next level. A tracking and analysis system could show which coupon offers are working and which are not, compare the amount of dealer revenue which is derived from each dollar invested in marketing, and specify the return on marketing investment derived from mailers targeted to different customers.

A variety of informational reports can be created by combining coupon redemption information with repair order information. For example, one report could show total repair order revenue generated by coupons redeemed. Another report could indicate repair revenue generated per marketing dollar invested, separated out according to owner's zip code, vehicle model year, and existing customers versus prospects. With the information from such reports, you can analyze the effectiveness of important components of the coupon mail program in order to improve future marketing strategies.

The charts below provide prototype examples of the kinds of information you could access.

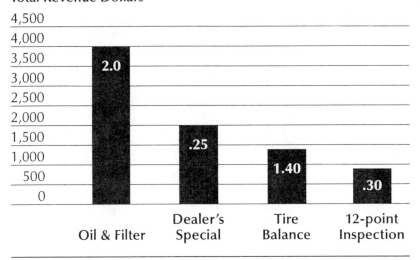

ABC Dealer One Month's Revenue Results

Response and Revenue by Type of Coupon Offer
(the numbers in the bars are response rates)

Total Revenue Dollars

	Oil & Filter	Dealer's Special	Tire Balance	12-point Inspection
response rate	2.0	.25	1.40	.30

Spring Coupon Redemption Report
Return on Investment (R.O.I.) by Model Year: National

Model Year Grouping	Total Revenue ÷	Marketing Expense (# of pieces mailed × cost per piece) =	Sales Revenue per Dollar Invested (R.O.I.)
0–3 years old	$ 861,300	$226,942	$3.8
4–7 years old	430,650	64,841	6.6
7+ years old	143,551	32,420	4.4
Totals	$1,435,501	$324,203	$4.4

Spring Coupon Redemption Report National and Regional Summary

Region/Number of Dealers	Dealers Participating in Mailing: % of All Dealers in Region	Dealers Sending Back Redeemed Coupons: % of All Dealers in Region	Total Coupons Redeemed: Overall Coupon Response Rate
Gulf (180)	126 (70%)	112 (62%)	2,913 (1.67%)
Western (110)	86 (78%)	66 (60%)	1,211 (1.10%)
Northwest (95)	68 (72%)	62 (65%)	1,426 (2.80%)
Northeast (135)	109 (81%)	94 (70%)	2,282 (1.65%)
Southeast (125)	78 (63%)	65 (52%)	3,253 (2.10%)
Midwest (141)	105 (74%)	93 (66%)	1,596 (2.80%)
Total/National (786)	572 (73%)	94 (63%)	12,681 (1.90%)

Tracking and analysis will provide valuable insights to corporate management and dealers in quantifying how effective direct marketing can be in improving dealership revenue and profitability. It will provide a foundation to begin a process of educating and training dealership managers to be more aggressive and effective in marketing their dealership for increased revenue. Initially, managers may not fully recognize or appreciate the value of tracking and analysis. However, over time it will become a critical component in quantifiably demonstrating the value of marketing and in guiding the program's effectiveness. Ultimately, this will lead to managers investing more dealership marketing dollars more effectively and increasing overall revenue.

Restaurant Case Study

This restaurant case study demonstrates how a fully integrated program of brand positioning, creative media planning, sales promotion, database marketing, and public relations more effectively launched the value initiative for Taco Bell.

In the mid 1980s, Taco Bell was struggling. The company did not meet sales and profit objectives, and its owner, PepsiCo, was pressing for better results. The company had plenty of room to grow. There were far fewer Taco Bell locations than McDonald's, Burger King, or Wendy's. Average Taco Bell sales per store were stalled at $525,000 per year in comparison to competitors' per-store sales averages of more than $1,000,000. There was plenty of growth potential. The question was how to tap that potential and build sales more rapidly.

Research Background

A number of research studies existed from which to start the process of understanding the customer's needs, wants, and motivational influences. The studies identified a group of people who frequently visited quick service restaurants and called this group heavy users.

Research showed that frequent users visit a quick service restaurant (QSR) 15 times per month. However, only two of those visits were to Taco Bell. The heavy-user customer represented one third of all QSR users, yet accounted for two thirds of all QSR visits. It is clear from this data that the greatest sales opportunity is the heavy-user customer segment. Considering that this customer group visited Taco Bell as part of a repertoire of restaurants, but much less frequently, this target segment of customers was the most promising for increasing sales.

Identifying the most profitable customer segment to focus on was the easy part. The next step was getting this customer segment to visit Taco Bell one more time per month, which could make a huge impact on sales. This became the biggest challenge for the company's marketing staff, to change frequent QSR customers' behavior to come to Taco Bell more often. To change behavior, first you have to analyze behavior. An analysis of several research studies laid the groundwork for truly understanding the heavy-user customer.

The research analysis showed that the most valuable attributes to the frequent QSR customer, ranked by importance, were:

1. Quick and convenient

2. Inexpensive and filling

3. Fresh ingredients and taste

These customers rated Taco Bell lower than competition for the quick and convenient, inexpensive and filling attributes, the very attributes the customer valued most. The good news was that Taco Bell ranked above competition for fresh ingredients and taste. Even though these were valued as third in importance, at least it was a starting point.

This was good data to begin formulating strategies for motivating the customer to visit Taco Bell more frequently. The focus should be on promoting Taco Bell as a superior value when value meant convenient, quick, inexpensive, filling, fresh ingredients, and taste.

This focus gave rise to a new set of challenges, to identify the best strategies and tactics to support the objective of a new brand image. It soon became clear that the convenient and quick attributes were as much an issue with the Taco Bell restaurant operations and new restaurant development departments as it was with the marketing department.

As a result, the marketing staff teamed up with the operation and restaurant development staffs. Within operations, discussion focused on increasing speed of service. With some serious soul-searching and analysis, it became clear that the problem was that restaurant staffs had a high turnover rate, and as a result, most restaurant staffs had inexperienced personnel. The easier their tasks could become, the faster they would be at serving customers. Together, the marketing and restaurant development departments determined the ideal number of restaurants for a given area of dominant influence, which is the market area covered by a TV signal. The ideal number to provide competitive marketplace presence turned out to be one restaurant for each 50,000 households. This, of course, was a long-term goal. Marketing could not wait for restaurant development to achieve the ideal market presence.

Research and analysis also revealed three additional key facts.

- Frequent QSR customers viewed the taco as the best value on the entire Taco Bell menu. This was significant because it was also the easiest and fastest for the staff to prepare.

- Tacos, when discounted to 49 or 59 cents, could increase heavy-QSR customer visits significantly. This was confirmed by a direct mail test sent to frequent QSR users that evaluated a variety of product price offerings and established the fact that tacos at 49 or 59 cents were the clear favorites over and above competitors' key products and prices.

- The company's profit margin for the taco was superior to all other menu items.

This was the foundation for building the marketing communications program. Customers would visit Taco Bell more often if offered low-priced tacos served quickly. Because the tacos were inexpensive, customers could buy more of them and be filled up inexpensively. From a competitive standpoint, analysis also revealed that McDonald's could not easily match the low price for tacos with similar products such as hamburgers and cheeseburgers. To break even with 49 cent tacos, transaction counts must increase by 20 percent. Anything above this would represent incremental profit.

The core issue of developing a successful marketing communications program was effective advertising of the new brand value images even with limited budgets. McDonald's out-spent Taco Bell by a four-to-one margin; Burger King out-spent Taco Bell by a two-to-one margin.

Mass Media

The Taco Bell value initiative strategy included several levels of marketing communication support. The foundation of the program was mass media. Mass media was a focus because of the broad nature of the target audience and the customer education process that was required. However, a key to the success of the value initiative strategy was in applying creativity, imagination, and experience to create maximum impact for the mass media program.

Another important aspect of the program's success was leveraging the mass media program to integrate other marketing communication elements to further enhance the overall program. This included sales promotion, sports marketing, direct response, and public relations.

With the key brand attributes firmly established, the brand's personality and image still needed definition. This was especially important because the purchase decision for the QSR customer is impulsive and driven by image and top-of-mind awareness. The QSR category was highly competitive and heavily advertised. The most relevant, appealing imagery would make the brand's advertising more memorable and effective in influencing the impulse purchase decision.

Research and market knowledge had indicated that Taco Bell's strengths were its different and fresher taste. This became the starting point for building the strategy. Focus group research helped fill out the picture. This consisted of conducting research interviews with heavy-QSR customers across the country. As part of the research interview, customers responded to questions about how they perceived Taco Bell versus McDonald's and other QSR brands. The bulk of the interview focused on getting customers to help profile the different QSR brands, including their perceptions of the positives and negatives of those brands. In the end, a clear picture emerged for the most relevant and effective brand personality for Taco Bell.

Customers perceived Taco Bell as more exciting, hip, and cool. It was the kind of place you would go if you were feeling a little adventurous. It was not mainstream like the other QSR brands. Taco Bell was more youthful and alive. There was nothing ordinary or boring about it. Taco Bell's image was a bit irreverent and somewhat rebellious. Since this was how the customer perceived Taco Bell, it was how they could best relate to, accept, and have positive feelings toward Taco Bell.

This customer input provided the additional information needed to finalize the strategy. The challenge was now for the ad agency to bring the strategy to life of hip food that is inexpensive and filling. It may sound easy, but it's not. The result was an advertising campaign called Run for the Border.

The campaign used music, people, a desert scene, unique props and outstanding food film to create the Taco Bell image. The music was high-energy, closer to what the customer would listen to for pleasure than typical commercial music.

The actors featured in the commercial were young, attractive, and real looking. These actors portrayed a unique border attitude, more confident, in-the-know, less inhibited than most. Usually, the selection of these actors was because this was their real attitude. It was difficult to act it. The attitude showed in the way they carried themselves, their expressions, and their outlook on life. Border people were born, not made, and they were instantly recognizable. This was one of the key elements that gave the advertising a unique edge.

Border people wanted to be different, and Taco Bell was the perfect solution to their everyday sameness. Taco Bell not only had better food, but it also broke the monotony of going to McDonald's every day. Taco Bell was the perfect escape place and escape food.

Usually when so much image and brand personality are portrayed in a commercial, there is little room left for the brand's other selling points. The Run for the Border campaign was an exception. It clearly and accurately registered the brand personality. By making the Taco Bell products and prices the real stars in the commercials, the entire message came through loud and clear.

Research results told the story. The commercial testing service awarded the commercials the highest scores in Taco Bell history. The in-market performance validated the research, with 25 to 30 percent sales gains every week. Despite this success, there was much more to the story than brand positioning strategy.

Local Media

At the time, the company's regional offices were responsible for all Taco Bell advertising planning and purchasing. Even though McDonald's out-spent Taco Bell by a wide margin, Taco Bell was in a better position to access the media marketplace on a local basis. The local strategies focused on high-profile sports sponsorships to better reach male customers, a large portion of frequent QSR customers. The sponsorships provided the leverage for building integrated marketing programs which included sales promotion, public relations, and direct mail.

This case study will follow the program for the Chicago market, one of Taco Bell's largest markets. This type of program was also used in other markets with appropriate modifications. While Taco Bell purchased several sports sponsorships throughout the year, the largest commitment was with the Chicago Bulls basketball team. The professional basketball season covers over half of the calendar year and thus offered many advertising opportunities.

The first step was to negotiate a comprehensive package with the Chicago TV station that broadcast the Bulls games. The package included the purchase of commercial air time throughout the season. This is where the TV station focused, because it was their primary revenue opportunity. To sign a sponsor with a large overall dollar commitment, stations will oftentimes include additional value-added marketing opportunities. The key is to present a very specific program idea to the station and gain agreement prior to actually committing media dollars.

The goal was to pay fair market value for the commercial air time and leverage this large dollar expenditure to get the additional marketing program elements included as part of the package. The deal consisted of the commercial air time, Taco Bell and Chicago Bulls promotional events, and bonus commercial time to advertise the promotional events.

The event created was called the Great Taco Bell Shoot-Out. In essence, the event was a basketball hoop shooting contest in which customers could win prizes by participating in local restaurant shoot-out contests. The customers filled out entry forms and deposited them in contest entry boxes at each restaurant. Randomly-selected customers then participated in each restaurant's local shoot-out contest. The best performers participated in the finals which aired during the Chicago Bulls' playoff games.

By positioning the Great Taco Bell Shoot-Out as a celebration of the new low prices at Taco Bell, the value strategy was the focus of all promotional activities. For example, 49-cent taco parties were a key part of the shoot-out prize pool. Additionally, greater prizes, such as free season tickets to the Bulls' games and trips to watch the Bulls in later playoff games, were integral prize pool elements. All of the shoot-out event posters included merchandising the new value prices. Also, the bonus commercials provided by the TV station to promote the event included the new price value message.

Concurrent with the launch of the value initiative strategy, the TV station provided several one-minute time blocks for interviews with Taco Bell executives. Interviews were conducted by Johnny 'Red' Kerr, the Bulls' long-time TV broadcaster, on the subject of the Great Taco Bell Shoot-Out and the new value pricing at Taco Bell. In total, the bonus commercials and the on-air interviews resulted in doubling the amount of commercial air time Taco Bell purchased, an excellent start to generating more bang-for-the-buck in launching the value initiative.

Customer entries from the shoot-out contests provided the basis to build a database and implement a relationship marketing program. Up until this point, Taco Bell did not have a database or relationship marketing program in place. The shoot-out contest entries provided an excellent place to start the database development process because these customers fit the QSR heavy-user profile. Furthermore, this customer group had taken steps to become involved with the Taco Bell brand, beyond eating occasions. To nurture loyalty and visit frequency among these key customers, Taco Bell implemented a relationship marketing program using direct mail.

Taco Bell also made a cash donation to the official Chicago Bulls' charity, the Charitabulls. The donation amount was tied to the total number of baskets made by the customer participants in the Shoot-Out event. Taco Bell managers presented a $21,000 check at center court during a Bull's playoff game. Press releases in local newspapers followed and were successful in securing favorable publicity for Taco Bell.

There were other media tactics to consider. To increase the media schedule's exposure and impact, 10-second commercials were included together with 30-second spots. The 10-second spots were incorporated into the schedule after the value strategy was established with the longer 30-second spots. This was the first time Taco Bell had used 10-second commercials, and they made a big difference in overall exposure for the new strategy.

Additionally, radio commercials became a part of the media plan for the first time. The purpose was to provide broader exposure for the value strategy, timely messages prior to lunch and dinner, and unique promotional exposure to make the media budget stretch even further. Since this was Taco Bell's first use of radio in this market, the radio stations were eager to get this new business and were all aggressively competitive to accommodate Taco Bell's needs. This was helpful in successfully negotiating extra promotional coverage at no additional cost.

The radio purchases included free air time for on-air giveaways and contests, which tied into the value strategy. Some examples of this were on-air giveaways of free taco lunches at Taco Bell scheduled during the lunch time shows which some radio stations aired. Other stations had on-air giveaways of taco parties, which were free tacos for 20 people.

The highest-rated radio program expanded the free taco parties idea into a South of the Border event. The disk jockeys took listeners to

Tijuana, Mexico, for a live broadcast of their show to celebrate Cinco De Mayo, the Mexican independence day. As part of the promotion leading up to this live broadcast, the station gave away taco parties on air. Several additional taco parties were given away on air the day of the actual Mexico broadcast. The disc jockeys had some fun with the taco party giveaways that added to the exposure and impact of the promotion for Taco Bell. The on-air promotional giveaways provided additional exposure of the Taco Bell value message at no cost to Taco Bell. In total, these on-air promotions generated nearly as much media exposure as the purchased schedule.

Point-of-sale Promotion

During the test phase of the value initiative strategy prior to the national launch, research indicated that sales would increase significantly — as much as double — if each restaurant used extensive point-of-sale material. The most effective place for the point-of-sale material was both inside and outside the restaurants. The critical thinking applied here was that the inside point-of-sale material helped to visually reinforce and firmly establish the value message to the customer. It also helped establish the new low prices as a new way of doing business, rather than a limited time promotion.

The purpose of the outdoor point-of-sale material was to provide additional exposure of the value message to both customers and prospective customers as they drove or walked past. The use of point-of-sale material took on a new meaning and led to expanding on the traditional point-of-purchase material of a mere flyer or poster. Entire point-of-sale kits were created that included carefully-designed roof banners, pole signs, window banners, ceiling danglers, door signs, and menu boards. Where allowed, the restaurants also used portable street signs and cardboard election signs. There were also custom-produced party packages that created a tone of excitement and celebration for the new low-price strategy and which included helium balloons, party streamers, banners, and piñatas.

Everyone went a little crazy to create the impression that there was something new and exciting at Taco Bell. The customers loved it because it gave them more of the feeling that Taco Bell was out-of-the-ordinary, a place they could escape to and break up the monotony of their day. The restaurant crews enjoyed it as well because it was fun and different. It helped increase morale and this, in turn, improved their speed of service. Everyone became excited. This was revolutionary, and everyone felt a part of it.

The local Taco Bell restaurant staffs were highly motivated. They actively promoted the value initiative by handing out fliers at nearby shopping centers and waving value signs to oncoming traffic in front of their restaurants. The more the restaurant crews did to promote the new value message, the more the restaurants' sales increased.

This type of merchandising and promotion became almost a sub-culture within the Taco Bell system that, to some extent, still exists today.

Program Execution

Implementing the new value strategy within a system the size of Taco Bell was a Herculean task, one that required extensive planning, communication, and follow-up. There were two aspects to the implementation plan, one for company-owned restaurants and one for franchised restaurants.

Company-owned restaurants made up 65 percent of the system. For these, Taco Bell management set up regional and district meetings with the local restaurant operation teams to explain the purpose and benefits of the new strategy and the expectation for their role in the process. Often this was a series of meetings that started with a large, marketwide rally which included all employees. As follow-up, the marketing staff issued detailed specifications for local restaurant promotion and merchandising activities and conducted in-store consultations. These were not one-time events. They occurred weekly and monthly to ensure that everyone understood the complete mission of the new strategy and to help them execute it as best they could.

Concurrently, a similar process was taking place with the system's franchised restaurants, but here the task was more difficult. Staff at franchises often displayed a cynical and skeptical attitude toward the parent corporation. A tremendous amount of explanation and justification was required to achieve cooperation from the franchise community which, in some regions, dominated the marketplace. The approach to each had to be different. In the markets where the company owned the majority of restaurants, the approach was to explain, justify, and hope the franchisees would buy in and support the program.

The franchisees were suspicious that the value strategy was a ploy by the company to increase sales and, therefore, increase the royalties that franchisees paid as a percentage of sales. The franchisees felt the company was doing this without regard for their net profit. They did believe the new strategy would be effective in generating increased sales but were skeptical of whether it would increase their bottom-line profits. In markets that franchisees dominated, the value initiative was delayed because the franchisees controlled the marketing funds and refused to play along.

Ultimately, the company controlled the marketing budgets, and the media plan was dictated by the company's strategy. This meant that all customers were receiving the value message via TV and radio. If franchisees did not participate in the new pricing strategy, they had a difficult time explaining it to the customers who came into their restaurants.

Over time, many franchisees tried the value strategy for themselves and experienced first-hand the positive results on sales and profit. These experiences proved crucial in that the franchisees who had these positive experiences would validate the value strategy to other franchisees. Once this happened, the franchise community began to follow suit and supported the company's value strategy.

Strategy Results

The results of the Taco Bell value initiative were extremely positive. The strategy and execution were successful in generating 20 to 30 percent sales and profit increases for a period of more than three years. It took this long for competitors to understand and implement value strategies of their own in response to Taco Bell.

This was due in large part to the way competitors franchised their restaurants. Most other quick service restaurant companies operated 90 percent or more of their restaurants as franchises. Consequently, they had much less control over implementing a value strategy because the majority of franchisees had to approve of it. Just like the Taco Bell franchisees, they were skeptical about the effect the plan would have on their bottom-line profits. Therefore, it took an even greater degree of justification and persistence before competitors could reach a consensus among their franchisees and gain approval to implement a value program. While this was occurring, competitors were losing market share and profits to Taco Bell.

Taco Bell had anticipated a slow response by competitors. This made the long-term potential of the value strategy even more attractive. In the end, nearly every competitor did implement their own version of the value strategy. As a result, restaurant marketing changed forever.

From these three different case studies you can see how an integrated communications marketing program can lead to success for your business. Some of the keys to this success for your brand are that you:

- Set marketing objectives based on analysis and understanding of your customers' needs, wants, and motivations.
- Review all possible marketing communication strategies and tactics, then use both discipline and creativity to select and apply the best combination of program components.
- Use marketing communication tactics as a means of collecting important, relevant customer information to build your customer database.
- Set quantifiable goals, measure program effectiveness, and refine programs over time to increase effectiveness.

Using the information and thought processes discussed in the preceding chapters will help guide you to design and implement your marketing communication programs. However, in the final analysis, the most effective marketing programs will depend on how well you can apply the processes described in this book in combination with creativity, experience, and judgment.

Chapter 6

Keep Track of Your Customers

Database Development

The purpose of this chapter is to explain the mechanics of developing a database, whether you develop it internally or help manage the process with an outside supplier. It also discusses statistical techniques to assist you in creating customer segments and selecting customers most likely to respond to a particular type of marketing communication.

Phase I – Building a Database

The database is a vital engine driving the development of more effective integrated marketing communication programs.

Some companies will have greater access and availability of detailed customer information than others. For example, quick service restaurants have a more difficult challenge collecting customer information than automotive companies because their transactions are in cash, and there are currently few, if any, point of sales tracking tools in use. On the other hand, automotive transactions are recorded and provide a great deal of valuable customer information. In any case, the challenge is to develop systems and tools that allow you to better collect and apply customer data. In nearly every case this can be accomplished.

The information collected in a database can provide you many opportunities to improve customer communication, measure effectiveness, and design more relevant and motivating marketing communication strategies and tactics. To be successful, you will need to invest the time and resources for building the database and for updating and maintaining it. The process is ongoing. As more information is collected, you can apply various methods to refine the information for superior application.

The following provides a detailed procedure for building a database using an automotive company as an example. While this may or may not be precisely parallel with your particular situation, it will provide relevant guidelines and principals for the overall database-building process.

Initial Preparation

The first step is to start with all of the owner file data to combine and standardize it into a workable format. This will include vehicle identification number (VIN), name, address, phone, and survey data. Then all records should be cleaned up to eliminate all duplicate records and update the owner name and address information. Update all the VINs by using state vehicle registration data in non-restricted states or using repair order information in restricted states. Add to the file any additional data available, such as other vehicles owned and previous vehicles owned.

To maintain control of costs, select a random sample of files to use in conducting preliminary segmentation. Use the results of this to determine what demographic information proves to be most relevant in grouping segments of owners. Then you would add these demographic characteristics to all owner files.

At this point you can produce a combined and cleansed data tape to conduct statistical analyses and customer segmentation. Write a detailed explanation of the processes and factors you used to arrive at these segments for later reference by other database users.

System Design

The best system design is a cooperative effort, requiring participation and input from all of the company's users, in order to optimize the database design and its applicability to your business needs.

Here are five steps to follow in the design process.

Step One: Needs Assessment

Begin with a disciplined inquiry intended to provide a detailed picture of what is expected of the system. Some factors to review include:

- Strategic and tactical requirements of your business,
- Sources and accuracy of available data,
- Current analytical and marketing information capabilities,
- A list of all prospective users, and
- Capabilities of the ultimate system the company wishes to build.

Step Two: Design Parameters

The process should continue with more detailed discussion of data content and system output needs. The object is to provide technical staff and systems analysts with a thorough understanding of these factors:

- The marketing data that will initially be entered into the system,
- Data likely to be added through upgraded processes or new data sources,
- Data elements to be combined through a process of summarization, aggregation, or calculation,
- The best way to handle repair data,
- The desired process for updating information and adding new information,
- Development and design of various database reports needed,
- The most frequently used tools of the system, such as for analysis or for producing lists, and
- What departments and staff will be using the database.

Step Three: Initial Design

The next step is to create the design for the database that will include all of the information available through internal resources and any data purchased from outside sources.

Step Four: Design Review

The database design should be reviewed with appropriate personnel for final modifications and approval.

Step Five: System Flexibility

The final step in system design is to determine how flexible the data structure is. The database structure should be flexible to accommodate future needs and changes over time. Therefore, it will be helpful to ask yourself some of the questions listed here, in order to make future changes and modifications easier.

- What additional data is likely to be added later?
- What other data sources are not presently included, such as other divisions?
- Are the procedures used for customer transactions likely to change over time?
- What future business plans might necessitate new informational needs, such as new vehicle makes and models?

If you have not already gotten involvement and input about the database design from other potential users in your company, now is the time to show them your design and get their suggestions before you begin creating files and then install the system.

File Creation

Once the system design is agreed upon, you can begin the actual process of creating customer files. Start by collecting data and information files from all your sources. A team of analysts should then match each available data element to the needs identified in the needs assessment step. Verify the data accuracy with the company's technical and marketing personnel. Programs must be written that will fit the raw data into the custom-formatted database. The accuracy of that programming is then thoroughly checked. Next, the database is constructed for the first time, and a series of intensive quality control checks are performed. Note that this step is not at the end of the process of file creation but at the beginning.

At this point, certain features can be added that will automatically standardize information as it is entered into the database so that you have a consistent format. Items you might want to standardize include:

- Address element
- First and last name separation
- Multiple name separation
- Name and address separation
- Multiple address line compaction

The core system is now complete and ready for the review of file accuracy. Any succeeding steps in the file creation process are designed to allow you to enrich the data for analyses or report purposes or enhance the database by adding custom-designed features.

Once all the files have been created and the final system built, the system is ready for installation. At this point, you should decide whether desktop tools are needed so that the system can be formatted for multiple user access.

Data Appending

In any data enhancement project, it is important to ensure the completeness of the data used. This usually requires using outside resources and vendors who can provide more customer data than you have from your own resources. This may include data such as income, credit rating, renter or home owner, and occupation. It is best to use a collection of all the vendor data sources available to provide the most complete combination of information possible.

Be aware that some customer-related data is not very reliable because it is changeable over time. Studies indicate that among common data elements such as age, income, home ownership, and length of residence, age is very accurate, home ownership and length of residence are fairly accurate, and income is not very accurate. One vendor's data shows that, while real estate data is not very reliable, it may be useful when combined with other data.

Incomplete Data Compensation

Even with the best combination of data, there will be holes that exist. There are ways to use modeling to fill in the blanks of a data set. The following gives an example of how modeling was used in this way to develop a database of automobile ownership across the entire nation.

To develop a national database of automobile ownership, the company was able to purchase motor vehicle data in 35 states. The other 15 states are prohibited by law from selling such information, due to privacy concerns. Rather than work with incomplete information, the company decided to estimate automobile ownership in those 15 states.

Here are the steps in the method used.

- The initial data set consisted of 10 million records from the 35 unrestricted states.
- Specific variables were selected from the entire 10 million records, which included demographics, lifestyle indicators, and data from motor vehicle departments.
- The resulting data set numbered 866,000 records. From these was pulled a training set of 650,000 records, leaving a holdout set of 216,000 records.
- Profiles, or models, were developed for each of several different car types, identifying segments of customers most likely to own a given car type.

The company used these actual models to estimate records from the other 15 states to create a larger data set of 20 million records. In the final result, the company was able to generate more than one million records of "most likely" car type owners.

Phase II – Customer Segmentation

Of possible strategies used to profile an automotive owner file, segmentation analyses often have the most merit. The important first step is to sort several like groups of customers into groups called segments. These groups are based on variables which would lead to more meaningful use of different types of custom marketing programs.

Customer segmentation is a much more useful method compared to historical approaches of creating target customer groups. Older methods fell short in that they created general groupings of individuals with no practical application. The same is true for other target segmentation methods which seek to define primary, secondary, and tertiary target segments based only on degree of category or brand usage. Frequently, they relied upon survey data which gives a snapshot of reported behavior but is not based on actual behavior.

An important advantage of custom segmentation is allowing for individuals to be moved from segment to segment over time. An example of this would be an individual in a segment of satisfied past owners who just purchased a new vehicle. This individual may be moved to a new segment, that of new owner, and placed in a different marketing program for service reminders, referrals, and relationship marketing.

When there is sufficient data, the broad customer segments can be subdivided even more specifically. The additional customer groups would then be cluster groups. The term cluster segmentation is used to describe a database that has many defined customer segments that are grouped in a methodical way. For example, you could divide past purchasers into cluster segments according to age category, such as 18–24, 25–34, 35–49 and so on. And you could further divide them according to past purchasers who are satisfied or who are not satisfied with their purchase choice.

Creating owner segments is the most effective approach for direct marketing application. Once this is established, you would then use modeling techniques to identify likely competitive make owners, to better target prospective customers.

What makes the customer segment approach useful is that it can be used in everyday strategy development. Once grouped, customers will be codified to make selections by segment as simple as possible. Also, the final output is quite simple to understand and apply.

Ultimately the goal of these marketing techniques is to influence customers' behavior to increase loyalty, repurchase, and use of the dealer for parts and service. A more sophisticated approach to customer segmentation will provide a better competitive advantage than does mass media, which is less precise in targeting specific customer types and also is far more costly. Ultimately, when used together, customer segments and custom-tailored marketing should have the greatest effectiveness and bang for the buck.

Data Validation

Data validation is extremely important for any marketing process but is especially necessary in the segmentation process. Specific data elements become the basis for a grouping. Hence, if the underlying data elements are unreliable, you have essentially built a house of cards. You can validate the data elements through survey methods that ask consumers specific questions to confirm the accuracy of elements such as age, income, occupation, and so on. This process will allow you to gauge the accuracy of all data elements.

Once the segments are created, this is the time for you to step in to determine their strategic appropriateness and knowledge enhancement. Strategic appropriateness means whether the clusters make sense and tie into your marketing strategy. Knowledge enhancement means in what ways can you add to your knowledge of your customers. You can add to this bank of knowledge by employing two techniques: focus groups and surveys.

Focus Groups

Conduct at least one focus group for each segment. This will provide a meaningful snapshot of who each segment really represents. This can also be a helpful orientation tool for your management team because sometimes actually seeing a segment of customers in person increases their understanding and buy-in.

Surveys

Send a survey to each customer segment to determine their attitudes, opinions, and interests on relevant topics. Again, using automotive as an example, a survey could gather such information as:

- Future vehicle purchase plans
- Attitudes towards financing options
- Service habits — do-it-yourselfers versus dealer patronage

- Whether the vehicle make is their primary or secondary auto
- Interest in receiving service coupon offers
- Media preferences

Incorporate New Information and Refine the Program

As you accumulate more information on customers, new variables are being added, which means you need to continue to analyze and refine the segments. Ongoing testing of various hypothetical marketing programs can provide new ways for defining the owner segments and the best marketing programs.

To measure the efficacy of the customer segments and the specialized marketing programs you developed, use a control group for comparison. The control group would consist of a random sample of non-segmented customers receiving the same stimuli as the specific customer segments. You then compare results from the customer segment groups and the control group. Results which are significantly higher in the test segment, relative to the control group, can be attributed to the effectiveness of defining the appropriate segment and your marketing communications.

Once you have established appropriate benchmarks, you can test new hypothetical variables against existing programs to determine even more effective segmentation and custom marketing programs. This is, of course, a continuing process to constantly improve and refine the program's results.

There are various questions to ask to begin in-depth analysis of your database. Can effective marketing programs be used for these customer segments? Is their purchasing behavior for service, parts, and new cars substantially different? Do they respond to mail or telemarketing in any significantly different manner? Which segments are the most cost-effective for marketing?

All of these questions and more will require you to develop a variety of test programs. The final portion of this chapter will highlight some major testing mechanisms. These are the RFM and FRAC models, regression analysis, neural networks, pattern recognition, and fractal analysis.

For additional reading on database marketing for the small business, read *TargetSmart* by Jay Newberg and Claudio Marcus.

Phase III – Analyze Your Database

There are a variety of systematic methods for refining the effectiveness of your database. Most rely on sophisticated mathematical analyses and computer processing. The methods described here are commonly used. The intent of these descriptions and discussions is to provide a working knowledge and understanding of how these techniques work.

The RFM and FRAC Models

As described by Bob Stone in his book, *Successful Direct Market Methods*, the RFM (recency, frequency, monetary) model can help you categorize and rate your customers. A point system is established based on a customer's purchases which are noted by quarter-years. A typical formula in its simplest form might be as this:

- Recency was listed as:

    24 points – bought in current quarter

    12 points – bought 4 to 6 months ago

    6 points – bought 7 to 9 months ago

    3 points – bought 10 to 12 months ago

- Frequency was the number of purchases times 4 points.
- Monetary was determined as 10 percent of each dollar purchase, with a ceiling of 9 points. The ceiling avoids distortion from an unusually large purchase.

Robert Kestenbaum has introduced a close alternative called the FRAC model. "F" represents frequency of purchase within a specified period. "R" is recency of purchase. "A" is amount of purchase followed by "C," the type of merchandise or service purchased. This last category, the type of product or service bought, often is an indicator of what that person is likely to buy in the future. In the FRAC model, frequency usually receives the most weight in points.

The RFM model provides a simple, straightforward means of adding up points and identifying the top point-earners as your best customers. The model can be developed using simple calculations. This model doesn't require an extensive database of many variables. Required data is limited to when a purchase was made, purchase frequency, and the value of the purchase. The FRAC model adds the additional variable of which service or product was purchased.

RFM produces acceptable results but is less predictive than more sophisticated techniques that examine more variables. There may be other important traits of your customers that are related to their inclination to buy which the RFM model does not touch on. Also, RFM deals with existing customers only, not prospects, therefore limiting its scope.

Regression Analysis

Regression analysis is a statistical technique that was developed in the 1920s and 1930s as a means of making accurate assumptions about people by examining a representative sample. Regression is designed to identify trends and central tendencies. Regression models assess which traits, such as demographic or behavioral for example, best predict future behavior. It is used by direct marketers as a modeling technique to help zero in on best prospects and customers. Regression allows the marketer to divide a mailing list or database into dozens or even hundreds of groups called cells, with each customer or prospect ranked on the basis of their probable performance.

Regression seeks to identify which variables from a data set best define an outcome, such as likelihood to respond. The selected variables are then incorporated into a mathematical formula to score each record for likelihood of response.

One of the most critical elements of regression analysis is selection of the variables to include in the model. Each available variable must be considered and its predictive power measured. Through extensive analysis, the variables are weighted and added together, and those that then provide the greatest predictive abilities are selected.

Many different approaches have been developed to identify the right set of predictive variables. One of the most common is called stepwise regression. Stepwise regression is a sophisticated modeling tool that allows one to work with a small sample of a large data set, then project results to the larger data set. It is extremely effective when only a limited amount of data is available for analysis.

Regression can best generate accurate predictions when a limited amount of information is known about individuals or when there are few interactions between the variables. For example, many direct marketers track only limited information about their customers, such as size of an order, kind of product ordered, or method of payment. They do not capture detailed demographic or credit-related information that would permit even more sophisticated modeling techniques. Regression provides an excellent prediction vehicle for such limited databases in which predictors combine in a simple additive fashion.

Regression analysis is a powerful technique but suffers from several major weaknesses. First, regression depends on several assumptions about the normality of the data and thus has difficulty incorporating data such as non-normal distributions, non-linear relationships, and missing values.

Second, regression uses an additive approach for determining the most predictive set of variables to include in the model. Regression is less effective at identifying the combinations of variables, called higher order interactions, that define an outcome. Often there are three, four, or five variables that alone are not very predictive, but together they prove to be extremely predictive. With a data set of 20 or more variables, regression has difficulty finding these variable combinations.

Third, regression produces only one stereotype solution. Modelers can get around that by further segmenting the data set by hand and may end up building several different models, but that's somewhat artificial.

Fourth, because regression works with samples of data, not the entire data set, it can be distorted by data that is not representative. Key decisions regarding which variables are included or omitted from the model depend on potentially minor differences in statistics; yet chance differences can have a major negative impact. For similar reasons, the model derived from the sample may not generalize well to the entire database population. Finally, regression may miss data nuances present in larger data sets that might lead to a higher level of prediction.

Neural Networks

A neural network is a technique that deduces information by looking at examples. Neural networks try to emulate the human brain's powerful ability to recognize patterns. The neural net can make a decision or a prediction by drawing on an inventory of patterns previously learned, seeking the one most relevant to the current situation.

Just as humans have brain neurons which are connected with synapses, neurals work with multiple inputs to derive a single conclusion. The network uses inputs, then weights and transforms them. Next it compares the fit to the desired outcome and amends the weights as necessary to come up with the optimal predictive model. This stage is completed on a training set of data, which is generally no more than 10,000 records.

Neurals learn by example and modify themselves, rather than having to be programmed with specific preconceived rules. Neural networks are capable of modeling complex data relationships without human intervention beyond data pre-processing.

There are several major advantages to neural networks. First is that, once a network is built, predictions or diagnostics can be completed extremely quickly, even ones of vast combinational complexity. Although the training phase is often time consuming, the execution phase can usually be completed more rapidly than with competing techniques. Accordingly, neurals are extremely well-suited for non-dynamic environments, such as in radar imaging for identifying friend versus foe and in cruise missile technology for terrain identification.

Second, neural networks can find multiple outcomes in a data set, compared to regression's search for a single stereotype. Neurals also will find combinations of variables for higher order interactions.

Third, unlike regression, neurals can work with non-normal distributions and missing values and can perceive patterns in cluttered, complex data.

Finally, neural networks can assess whether the data set being used is sufficient to address the business problem. If a good model is not generated by the neural network, it is more likely due to insufficient data than to an insufficient system.

While neural networks represent a major advancement in modeling, they have limitations. First, neurals take a long time to train. This means that in a dynamic environment, model updates can be exceedingly time-consuming. Models must be rebuilt from scratch, or a large number of new cases must be submitted to the neural network to overcome results developed from previous cases.

A second limitation is that most neural networks are trained using 10,000 to 20,000 file records. Just as with regression, this sampling approach may miss nuances present in the complete set of data. For example, one of neural network's advantages is its ability to uncover combinations of variables. However, when you are looking for interactions of four, five, or six variables, the particular set of values that show a particular effect may not occur as frequently in the sample as they might in the entire database.

The third and perhaps the most common complaint about neurals is it is often unclear why a neural network works in a given situation. Unlike regression or other techniques, the variables making up the model are not explicitly presented. If the neural doesn't produce an optimal result, it's difficult to establish theories on what to try next. Some neural modelers argue that it is not a mysterious process because neurals use standard mathematical and statistical techniques. However, others believe that this fact does not compensate for a lack of understanding of why it works or does not work in a given situation.

Pattern Recognition

Pattern recognition is a modeling approach that searches through entire data sets to uncover patterns related to a specific outcome. It identifies distinctly different subgroups of individuals, with each group identified by a unique combination of variables. The pattern recognition approach does not necessarily refer to recognition of actual consumer activity, though this is possible, but rather to patterns that exist among groups, such as combinations of demographic or behavioral variables. Nuances and correlations among many variables can be identified, including those beyond human cognitive ability to uncover. This can result in extremely predictive models.

The theory of pattern recognition has been in existence for years, but it has taken the development of powerful and accessible computers combined with efficient search algorithms to bring the technology from theory to practice. The search algorithms have a foundation in computer chess, which necessitates searching through an extraordinarily large number of possible move combinations. The technology is a major enhancement of a previous method called CART (Classification And Regression Trees). Pattern recognition applies splitting algorithms to differentiate a population based on a given outcome. Instead of the CART approach of looking for a single variable, pattern recognition develops combinations of up to seven variables.

The pattern recognition approach looks for segments of the database population that rank high on the outcome variable and that are defined by a common set of characteristics. By searching through the entire data set and testing vast numbers of possible variable combinations, the approach first identifies a top segment, for example a group with the highest response level. This segment is put aside, another segment is identified and pulled out, and the process repeats until the entire data set is segmented. The process begins to resemble that of an upside down tree. Each of the end boxes, called leaves, represent a segment of the database, such as a group of households, related to the model outcome.

Pattern recognition has several distinct advantages. First, the analysis is completed on the entire data, not just a sample or subset of data, thus capturing subtle nuances that sampling can miss. In fact, pattern recognition's accuracy actually improves with larger data sets, due to increased data density. Second, the use of combinations of variables, compared to regression's additive approach, vastly improves the accuracy of the models. Third, pattern recognition can work effectively with data sets of non-normal distribution and with imprecise or missing data.

In pattern recognition, unlike neurals, the variables and values defining each segment are clearly defined and explainable. The rules used to form and group models are explicitly presented. Also, no assumptions have to be made about the data or which variables to include; instead, the relevant variables are identified by the search algorithms.

In addition, pattern recognition uses an approach which is particularly good at examining the tail ends of a distribution, such as those persons most likely to purchase an expensive item, or those persons likely not to pay their bills. Although these individuals may represent a mere five percent of your customer population, identifying them may be critical to solving a business problem.

Finally, the pattern recognition method retains all the information that resides in the database: all observations, all experiences, and all patterns. As a result, pattern recognition is dramatically different from more traditional methods in which rules are applied to a sample of data as an abbreviated summary of the original data. In contrast, pattern recognition has the ability to work with many variables at the same time and can recognize relationships and interactions in the data that are usually missed by other methods. No information is lost. Therefore, pattern recognition is an exceptionally powerful tool for use in two key activities for marketers, forecasting and segmentation.

Because pattern recognition searches for relationships and interactions between variables, a certain minimum amount of data is required. The approach does not work well on data sets of under 25,000 records nor on larger data sets with a limited number of variables.

Secondly, pattern recognition is not well-suited for analysis of data sets with limited information for each record, such that interactive effects are absent.

Fractals

Fractal geometry provides the basis for an ability to recognize patterns in seeming chaos. Fractals work on the assumption that data conforms to discernible patterns and that if one looks at a small bit of data and finds the patterns, the whole picture will emerge as a larger version of the smaller. The approach is similar to comparing the vessel structure on a leaf to the branch structure and to the entire root system of a tree.

The idea of fractals is that there are very basic structures that can be put together to form very complex structures. It is similar to the Russian wooden craft which puts an egg inside of an egg inside of an egg inside of an egg. Fractals start with simple components, looking first at the detail of a tiny structure. The same pattern is then used to structure the next stage and the intermediate stage and the global stage, all composing a complex structure.

One can also use fractal analysis to look at complex structures and through a reverse process find the underlying pattern and characteristics. It is in essence a data compression technique. Fractals can compress numerical summaries of very large databases into small files. If you have a lot of complex data, one of the ways of compacting and compressing it would be to use fractal-type arrangements. With a lot of raw numbers, such as in a large database, the fractal approach assumes that there are some underlying, inherent structures that could be captured by a fractal representation. You could make the entire database 1/100th of its size, using fractal analysis, and thus better understand it.

Fractals open up new capabilities because the compact and self-organized interactions make extremely multidimensional views possible, views that can be manipulated across any variable or set of variables. Fractal geometry produces a non-linear, multivariate analysis for creating a model.

The fractal approach does not employ standard statistical techniques; no sampling or top-end limit on the amount of historical data is required. A key factor is that it is not a sampling procedure. It makes use of all data from every record.

Fractal compression technology increases storage efficiency, making it possible to store up to a billion counts and associated indices on a standard computer hard drive.

Fractal analysis has limitations. Because fractals assume an underlying structure and try to fit the world into that structure, selection of variables remains a decision of major importance. You will have to be certain that the variables selected provide sufficient predictive ability.

A second issue is that the analytical approach omits a lot of detail. Look at whether the detail lost was unimportant anyway or rather something significant, then decide whether you can afford to lose the detail.

Also, for some data sets, a fractal model may not be a true representation of the underlying structure.

Statistical analysis and modeling can be valuable tools to assist in improving the effectiveness of your database. It is highly technical and complex; therefore, you will generally want to consult with experts specializing in this particular field.

In developing these tools, you should apply experience and judgment as it relates to marketing your particular brand.

Keeping track of your customers and adding to your knowledge of customer needs and behavior is the most important principle of effective integrated marketing communication. When your database is refined and enhanced with up-to-date customer information on a continual basis, it will provide you the necessary information to implement highly effective marketing programs. However, it is just as important that you design those programs to continuously gather accurate new information for your database. In this way you can truly improve your knowledge of your customer.

Chapter 7

Keep Abreast of Technology

What Lies Ahead

The successful application of new marketing techniques could evolve and grow with technology and human creativity.

New marketing techniques will not be solely dependent on technology. Rather new and effective techniques will be developed by harnessing and applying technology in new and different ways. Human creativity will drive marketing program effectiveness to new levels.

This will come about as marketing practitioners become more knowledgeable and comfortable in working with the many direct response and interactive techniques available. This knowledge will allow new thinking and ideas to be used.

The possibilities for new and creative applications are endless, once you begin looking at what is and wondering what could be. This will occur with professionals observing the marketing landscape that exists around them and imaging how new ideas and technics can be used for greater effectiveness.

Marketing in the new millennium will be different in that all forms of marketing communications will become interactive. The walls will come down between conventional mass media as a one-way communication and direct response as a dialogue. Through mass media, direct response, and new forms of interactive marketing communication, people will seek to establish an ongoing dialogue with customers. Through this dialogue, more and more customer information will be accumulated and better, more specialized information will be available to customers.

Information will become big in this new paradigm. Customers will place greater values on communication that provides useful information to help enrich their lives.

Imagine the day when real estate agents create a custom Web site for each and every one of their customers. The Web site would have a profile of the vital information desired about the real estate transaction process, customized for each customer. Then the customer's own Web site could be updated with information uniquely relevant to their needs, whether it be mortgage rates and programs, school locations, average home prices, or new listings. The customer could access their information, on their own Web site, at their convenience, and all of the information would be uniquely customized for them.

Or, imagine an individual Web site created for tracking the repair and maintenance of your vehicle. Based on your specific vehicle make and your driving habits, reminders of services needed are sent to you by e-mail. Additionally, you would have a complete history of all repair and maintenance ever performed, electronically accessed through your own computer.

The important message to be learned is that creativity and imagination are the valuable assets necessary to harness and apply new technologies and marketing techniques in the new millennium. This can be accomplished by understanding the variety of marketing communication techniques available and applying these techniques in new ways that are relevant and more effective to your business. This will result in greater productivity of your marketing expenditures and, ultimately, better business results.

Good luck marketing in the new millennium!

Index

From The Leading Publisher of Small Business Information
Books that save you time and money.

"Sales," writes author Stan Lindsay, "is nothing more that the term persuasion with the added implication that a proposed monetary exchange is involved. Persuasion, he explains in his approach, is not necessarily an unethical pursuit. Based on this philosophy, the author identifies 21 compenents of a sale and shows how to pursue them chronologically to a successful conclusion.

The Twenty-One Sales in a Sale   **Pages: 240**
Paperback: $19.95   ISBN: 1-55571-448-X

This sales training guide is specifically for those selling expensive items and interacting face-to-face with consumers. It explains how to employ a winning approach even when stakes are high,and gives insights into patterns of buying exclusive products, so that the seller has a greater sense of comfort through the sales process and exercises more control over its outcome. Author Hal Slater speaks from experience as a three-time recipient of General Motors' highest sales award.

Secrets to High-Ticket Selling   **Pages: 200**
Paperback: $19.95   ISBN: 1-55571-422-6

This hands-on, practical marketing guide will take you step-by-step from launching a new product to acquiring and keeping a core of satisfied-plus customers. It gives you a comprehensive set of marketing tools and strategies, including the worksheets necessary to help you develop a successful marketing plan.

Marketing Mastery   **Pages: 200**
Paperback: $19.95   ISBN: 1-55571-357-2

With the immense popularity of the Internet, many businesses and organizations are feeling the pressure to establish some sort of Internet presence. *Connecting Online* cuts through the hype and shows you why it is essential to first establish a solid image and communicative environment with your key audiences on the Internet. This book is the definitive source for all of your image building strategies on the Internet, regardless of whether you are a seasoned professional or entirely new to the concept.

Connecting Online   **Pages: 470**
Paperback: $21.95   ISBN: 1-55571-403-X

From The Leading Publisher of Small Business Information
Books that save you time and money.

If you've ever wondered how to combine business success and personal significance, author Gerald Baron has some practical suggestions. After years of working with executives and entrepreneurs, he's found that business success and personal meaning can share a common ground. Using dozens of real-world examples, he shows hwo building relationships is the key to business development and personal fulfillment.

Friendship Marketing   **Pages: 183**
Paperback: $18.95   **ISBN: 1-55571-399-8**

The heart of customer service — the transaction between customer and service provider — is the focus of this book. Author Richard Gallagher demonstrates how the three secrets of customer service make these transactions satisfying and productive. An excellent follow-up to Stan Lindsay's *The Twenty-One Sales in a Sale*!

Smile Training Isn't Enough   **Pages: 200**
Paperback: $19.95   **ISBN: 1-55571-422-6**

Many small business' avoid advertising, for fear that they could risk thousands of dollars on the wrong advertising decisions. This guide will assist anyone contemplating advertising and give the reader the low-down on each advertising medium available to business owners. Author Kathy Kobliski provides the basics on pinpointing customer markets, identifying the best way to communicate with that audience, as well as several other critical aspects of advertising successfully.

Advertising Without An Agency   **Pages: 200**
Paperback: $19.95   **ISBN: 1-55571-429-3**

As marketing goes increasingly global, CEOs and sales-and-marketing execs are scrambling to keep up — to position their products correctly in the international marketplace, or just to begin exploring sales avenues outside of the United States. *Developing International Markets* is ideal for anyone interested in this arena. It provides information on what to expect, how to avoid fruitless marketing activities, how to find local marketing agents, plus it covers the requirements that are often overlooked.

Developing International Markets   **Pages: 340**
Paperback: $19.95   **ISBN: 1-55571-433-1**

The Oasis Press® Order Form

MFNM4/98

Call, Mail, Email, or Fax Your Order to: PSI Research, P.O. Box 3727, Central Point, OR 97502
Email: sales@psi-research.com   Website: http://www.psi-research.com
Order Phone USA & Canada: +1 800 228-2275   Inquiries & International Orders: +1 541 479-9464 Fax: +1 541 476-1479

TITLE	✔ BINDER	✔ PAPERBACK	QUANTITY	COST
Advertising Without An Agency		❏ $19.95		
Bottom Line Basics	❏ $39.95	❏ $19.95		
BusinessBasics: A Microbusiness Startup Guide		❏ $17.95		
The Business Environmental Handbook	❏ $39.95	❏ $19.95		
Business Owner's Guide to Accounting & Bookkeeping		❏ $19.95		
Buyer's Guide to Business Insurance	❏ $39.95	❏ $19.95		
California Corporation Formation Package	❏ $39.95	❏ $29.95		
Collection Techniques for a Small Business	❏ $39.95	❏ $19.95		
A Company Policy and Personnel Workbook	❏ $49.95	❏ $29.95		
Company Relocation Handbook	❏ $39.95	❏ $19.95		
CompControl: The Secrets of Reducing Worker's Compensation Costs	❏ $39.95	❏ $19.95		
Complete Book of Business Forms		❏ $19.95		
Connecting Online: Creating a Successful Image on the Internet		❏ $21.95		
Customer Engineering: Cutting Edge Selling Strategies	❏ $39.95	❏ $19.95		
Develop & Market Your Creative Ideas		❏ $15.95		
Developing International Markets		❏ $19.95		
Doing Business in Russia		❏ $19.95		
Draw The Line: A Sexual Harassment Free Workplace		❏ $17.95		
Entrepreneurial Decisionmaking		❏ $19.95		
The Essential Corporation Handbook		❏ $21.95		
the Essential Limited Liability Company Handbook	❏ $39.95	❏ $21.95		
Export Now: A Guide for Small Business	❏ $39.95	❏ $24.95		
Financial Decisionmaking: A Guide for the Non-Accountant		❏ $19.95		
Financial Management Techniques for Small Business	❏ $39.95	❏ $19.95		
Financing Your Small Business		❏ $19.95		
Franchise Bible: How to Buy a Franchise or Franchise Your Own Business	❏ $39.95	❏ $24.95		
Friendship Marketing: Growing Your Business by Cultivating Strategic Relationships		❏ $18.95		
Funding High-Tech Ventures		❏ $21.95		
Home Business Made Easy		❏ $19.95		
Information Breakthrough		❏ $22.95		
The Insider's Guide to Small Business Loans	❏ $29.95	❏ $19.95		
InstaCorp – Incorporate In Any State (Book & Software)		❏ $29.95		
Joysticks, Blinking Lights and Thrills		❏ $18.95		
Keeping Score: An Inside Look at Sports Marketing		❏ $18.95		
Know Your Market: How to Do Low-Cost Market Research	❏ $39.95	❏ $19.95		
The Leader's Guide		❏ $19.95		
Legal Expense Defense: How to Control Your Business' Legal Costs and Problems	❏ $39.95	❏ $19.95		
Location, Location, Location: How to Select the Best Site for Your Business		❏ $19.95		
Mail Order Legal Guide	❏ $45.00	❏ $29.95		
Managing People: A Practical Guide		❏ $21.95		
Marketing for the New Millennium: Applying New Techniques		❏ $19.95		
Marketing Mastery: Your Seven Step Guide to Success	❏ $39.95	❏ $19.95		
The Money Connection: Where and How to Apply for Business Loans and Venture Capital	❏ $39.95	❏ $24.95		
Moonlighting: Earn a Second Income at Home		❏ $15.95		
People Investment	❏ $39.95	❏ $19.95		
Power Marketing for Small Business	❏ $39.95	❏ $19.95		
Profit Power: 101 Pointers to Give Your Business a Competitive Edge		❏ $19.95		
Proposal Development: How to Respond and Win the Bid	❏ $39.95	❏ $21.95		
Raising Capital		❏ $19.95		
Renaissance 2000: Liberal Arts Essentials for Tomorrow's Leaders		❏ $22.95		
Retail in Detail: How to Start and Manage a Small Retail Business		❏ $15.95		
Secrets to High Ticket Selling		❏ $19.95		
Secrets to Buying and Selling a Business		❏ $24.95		
Secure Your Future: Financial Planning at Any Age	❏ $39.95	❏ $19.95		
The Small Business Insider's Guide to Bankers		❏ $18.95		
SmartStart Your (State) Business... series		❏ $19.95		
PLEASE SPECIFY WHICH STATE(S) YOU WANT:				
Smile Training Isn't Enough: The Three Secrets to Excellent Customer Service		❏ $19.95		
Start Your Business (Available as a book and disk package)		❏ $ 9.95 (without disk)		

BOOK SUB-TOTAL (Additional titles on other side)

TITLE	✔ BINDER	✔ PAPERBACK	QUANTITY	COST
Starting and Operating a Business in...series *Includes FEDERAL section PLUS ONE STATE section*	❑ $34.95	❑ $27.95		
PLEASE SPECIFY WHICH STATE(S) YOU WANT:				
STATE SECTION ONLY (BINDER NOT INCLUDED) SPECIFY STATE(S):	❑ $8.95			
FEDERAL SECTION ONLY (BINDER NOT INCLUDED)	❑ $12.95			
U.S. EDITION (FEDERAL SECTION – 50 STATES AND WASHINGTON DC IN 11-BINDER SET)	❑ $295.95			
Successful Business Plan: Secrets & Strategies	❑ $49.95	❑ $27.95		
Successful Network Marketing for The 21st Century		❑ $15.95		
Surviving Success		❑ $19.95		
TargetSmart! Database Marketing for the Small Business		❑ $19.95		
Top Tax Saving Ideas for Today's Small Business		❑ $16.95		
Twenty-One Sales in a Sale: What Sales Are You Missing?		❑ $19.95		
Which Business? Help in Selecting Your New Venture		❑ $18.95		
Write Your Own Business Contracts	❑ $39.95	❑ $24.95		
BOOK SUB-TOTAL (Be sure to figure your amount from the previous side)				

OASIS SOFTWARE   Please specify which computer operating system you use (DOS, MacOS, or Windows)

TITLE	✔ Windows	✔ MacOS	Price	QUANTITY	COST
California Corporation Formation Package ASCII Software	❑	❑	$ 39.95		
Company Policy & Personnel Software Text Files	❑	❑	$ 49.95		
Financial Management Techniques (Full Standalone)	❑		$ 99.95		
Financial Templates	❑	❑	$ 69.95		
The Insurance Assistant Software (Full Standalone)	❑		$ 29.95		
Start Your Business (Software for Windows™)	❑		$ 19.95		
Successful Business Plan (Software for Windows™)	❑		$ 99.95		
Successful Business Plan Templates	❑	❑	$ 69.95		
The Survey Genie - Customer Edition (Full Standalone)	❑ $199.95 (WIN)	❑ $149.95 (DOS)			
The Survey Genie - Employee Edition (Full Standalone)	❑ $199.95 (WIN)	❑ $149.95 (DOS)			
SOFTWARE SUB-TOTAL					

BOOK & DISK PACKAGES Please specify which computer operating system you use (DOS, MacOS, or Windows)

TITLE	✔ Windows	✔ MacOS	✔ Binder	✔ Paperback	QUANTITY	COST
The Buyer's Guide to Business Insurance w/ Insurance Assistant	❑		❑ $ 59.95	❑ $ 39.95		
California Corporation Formation Binder Book & ASCII Software	❑	❑	❑ $ 69.95	❑ $ 59.95		
Company Policy & Personnel Book & Software Text Files	❑	❑	❑ $ 89.95	❑ $ 69.95		
Financial Management Techniques Book & Software	❑		❑ $129.95	❑ $ 119.95		
Start Your Business Paperback & Software (Software for Windows™)	❑			❑ $ 24.95		
Successful Business Plan Book & Software for Windows™	❑		❑ $125.95	❑ $109.95		
Successful Business Plan Book & Software Templates	❑	❑	❑ $109.95	❑ $ 89.95		
BOOK & DISK PACKAGE SUB-TOTAL						

AUDIO CASSETTES

	✔ Paperback	QUANTITY	COST
Power Marketing Tools For Small Business	❑ $ 49.95		
The Secrets To Buying & Selling A Business	❑ $ 49.95		
AUDIO CASSETTES SUB-TOTAL			

Sold To: **Please give street address**

NAME: _____

Title: _____

Company: _____

Street Address: _____

City/State/Zip: _____

Daytime Phone: _____ Email: _____

Ship To: **If different than above, please give alternate street address**

NAME: _____

Title: _____

Company: _____

Street Address: _____

City/State/Zip: _____

Daytime Phone: _____

Your Grand Total

SUB-TOTALS (from other side)	$
SUB-TOTALS (from this side)	$
SHIPPING (see chart below)	$
TOTAL ORDER	$

If your purchase is:	Shipping costs within the USA:
$0 - $25	$5.00
$25.01 - $50	$6.00
$50.01 - $100	$7.00
$100.01 - $175	$9.00
$175.01 - $250	$13.00
$250.01 - $500	$18.00
$500.01+	4% of total merchandise

04/98

Payment Information: **Rush service is available, call for details.**
International and Canadian Orders: Please call for quote on shipping.

☐ CHECK Enclosed payable to PSI Research   Charge: ☐ VISA   ☐ MASTERCARD   ☐ AMEX   ☐ DISCOVER

Card Number: _____ Expires: _____

Signature: _____ Name On Card: _____